Punishment and Politics

Punishment and Politics

Evidence and Emulation in the Making of English Crime Control Policy

---

by Michael Tonry

Published by

Willan Publishing
Culmcott House
Mill Street, Uffculme
Cullompton, Devon
EX15 3AT, UK
Tel: +44(0)1884 840337
Fax: +44(0)1884 840251
e-mail: info@willanpublishing.co.uk
website: www.willanpublishing.co.uk

Published simultaneously in the USA and Canada by

Willan Publishing
c/o ISBS, 920 NE 58th Ave, Suite 300
Portland, Oregon 97213-3786, USA
Tel: +001(0)503 287 3093
Fax: +001(0)503 280 8832
e-mail: info@isbs.com
website: www.isbs.com

First published 2004

ISBN 1-84392-063-8 (hardback)
ISBN 1-84392-062-X (paperback)

British Library Cataloguing-in-Publication Data
A catalogue record for this book is available from the British Library

Project management by Deer Park Productions,Tavistock, Devon
Typeset by GCS, Leighton Buzzard, Beds
Printed and bound by T.J. International, Padstow, Cornwall

Contents

Preface

Why is England the only major Western country whose government has chosen to emulate American crime-control policies and politics of the past quarter century?

It is puzzling.

During the 1970s and 1980s, England suffered from the same steeply rising crime rates that all Western countries did. And during the 1990s, England like other Western countries enjoyed sharply declining crime rates. Throughout the Western world, and in Eastern Europe, crime rates fell, whether imprisonment rates were high or low, rising or falling; whether police styles were traditional or innovative; whether nationwide crime-prevention initiatives were extensive or nonexistent. No matter what governments did or didn't do, crime rates fell.

Since the 1980s, many senior English practitioners, policy analysts and researchers have agreed, with their counterparts throughout Europe, that punishment practices and imprisonment patterns have little effect on crime rates and trends. Those are caused by broad-based social, economic and normative changes and the power of primary socializing institutions like families, schools and churches. In Labour's 'tough on crime, tough on the causes of crime' mantra, it's the causes that matter.

And yet in 2004, England has implemented Europe's only 'three-strikes-and-you're-out law' and American-style mandatory minimum sentence laws. Earlier it experimented with boot camps and zero-tolerance policing. England's government employs the most hyperbolic anti-crime rhetoric of any in Europe, language that elsewhere characterizes xenophobic right-wing fringe parties. Blair, Le Pen and Fortuyn are an odd and unexpected trio.

England has the highest imprisonment rate in Europe and the most rapidly rising prison population. And Parliament late in 2003 enacted a Criminal Justice Act full of symbolic tough-on-crime measures, some of which are sure more often to result in wrongful convictions of innocent people.

Since the 1980s, many senior English practitioners, policy analysts and researchers have celebrated, with their counterparts throughout Europe, the expansion of procedural protections of human rights in the criminal justice system. And yet the Criminal Justice Act 2003 is bedecked with provisions withdrawing and weakening procedural protections afforded people accused of crimes.

A possible reason why England alone is emulating the United States is that American policies have been marvellously successful, but somehow only English policy-makers have noticed. This isn't and can't be true.

Many of the most notorious American innovations, including some that England has embraced and others it has considered, have been conspicuously unsuccessful, and at devastating social and economic cost. Most informed people across the American political spectrum accept that three-strikes, mandatory minimum and truth-in-sentencing laws have had few if any crime-reduction effects. They have, however, produced unjustly severe punishments, ballooned the prison population, and, once enacted, proven remarkably hard to repeal.

Similarly, most informed observers now recognize that zero-tolerance policing had little to do with New York City's crime-rate declines in the 1990s (most other large American cities enjoyed similar declines whatever their policing styles), but resulted in large increases in police violence, racial confrontation, and unnecessary imprisonment.

American policies have had enormous, widely acknowledged costs – much the highest imprisonment rate among Western countries, the lengthiest prison sentences in the world, increasing numbers of executions, a third of its young black men under criminal justice system supervision, an iatrogenic 'War on Drugs' and unhappy recognition in many states that prisons are receiving vast sums that would be better spent on education or health care.

All across the United States, judges, prosecutors, and legislators are changing direction. Mandatory minimum and three-strikes laws are much less often invoked. States are repealing tough laws, releasing people from prison earlier and creating new drug treatment and other policies meant to divert people from prison.

I am confident that most senior civil servants in the Home Office agree with much of what I've said in the preceding paragraphs – it's a fair summary of the policy and research literatures, and of recent American developments – and have themselves said similar things to ministers. Ministers have refused to listen.

The current Labour government has knowingly adopted policies known to be ineffective or unlikely to work because of an arguable belief that its own continuation in office justifies the unnecessary human suffering and waste of public resources that its policies produce.

Policy-makers adopt bad policies for four kinds of reasons – evidence, ignorance, ideology and self-interest. Sometimes they believe, wrongly but honestly, that existing evidence gives valid reasons to believe that policies will have wanted effects. Sometimes they act ignorantly, simply not knowing that what seems a good idea isn't. Sometimes they are so influenced by ideology or political self-interest that they adopt policies primarily for symbolic reasons, without knowing or caring whether they will work.

The last is what happened in England. Deliberate decisions to emulate harsh American crime-control policies in general, and Bill Clinton's political approach to crime ('Don't let your opponents look tougher than you do') in particular, are among the results. So are sky-rocketing prison populations, worsening racial disparities, demoralized officials and avoidable suffering by offenders, their loved ones and their communities.

To an American, resident now in England for five years, who long admired the rationality, decency and moderation of England's criminal justice system, especially in comparison with the United States, all that I have described is perplexing. Until the early 1990s only America developed an hyperbolic law-and-order politics and cruel, simplistic policies that were based more on ideology and politicians' perceived self-interest than on evidence or acceptance of human frailty. And then in the early 1990s, England broke ranks with other Western countries and began to emulate American politics and policies.

Why, I wondered, and with what effects?

In this book, I attempt to disentangle the influences of evidence, ignorance, ideology and self-interest in New Labour's crime policies and its recent proposals for changes to the criminal justice system. In the first half, I examine central proposals in the recent White Paper *Justice for All* and the ensuing 2002 Criminal Justice Bill and 2003

Criminal Justice Act, and related rhetoric and political symbolism, and then consider why English crime policy has evolved as it has. Tony Blair's decision to follow the lead of Bill Clinton's New Democratic Coalition is the answer, but that leads to the deeper questions of why that seemed necessary or why it worked.

The second half looks at policy proposals and developments on three key subjects – sentencing, violence, racial disparities – and considers how they stack up against available experience and research evidence, and, if important policy goals are genuinely sought to be achieved, how that might best be done.

Acknowledgements

Most of what we know, we learn from other people. In writing this book, I've benefited from numerous statistical and policy reports published by the Home Office and from the work of innumerable British, European, and American scholars of crime and criminal justice. In particular, I've learned from the writings on English criminal justice policy making of Andrew Ashworth, Anthony Bottoms, David Downes, Ian Dunbar, David Faulkner, David Garland, Anthony Langdon, Rod Morgan, Tim Newburn, Mick Ryan, and David Windlesham. A number of friends read earlier drafts – Elizabeth Burney, David Downes, David Faulkner, Amanda Matravers, Tim Newburn, Nicky Padfield, Andrew von Hirsch, and Lorraine Waterhouse. All offered leads and advice and tried to save me from error and misjudgement. Amanda Matravers applied her red editor's pen to an earlier draft, and tried to save me from grosser infelicities of style. She kindly allowed me to base chapter 4 on an essay we earlier wrote together. David Green searched out the newspaper sources relied on in the text and several of the tables. Sara Harrop, already an editorial legend in her short time at the Cambridge Institute of Criminology, helped with nearly everything, including jacket design and artwork, references, figures and tables, and, inevitably not entirely successfully, adaptation of my colonial style, vocabulary, and spelling to British conventions. However imperfect the final product, it is better for all these people's help, and I am gratefully in their debt.

Chapter 1

Evidence

Crime-control policy in England and Wales of late has been tumultuous and schizophrenic. The tumult is evidenced by the following observation in the Halliday report, the foundation document on which the Criminal Justice Act 2003 builds:

> The onus is on those who propose change to show that it would be worthwhile. That is especially so after a decade that has seen more change in this field than any other in living memory. Many ... have expressed frustration over apparently incessant and disconnected changes, and pessimism about the likelihood that further changes will be beneficial.
>
> (Home Office 2001b: 1)

The schizophrenia is seen in the sometimes startling contrast between the Labour government's claim to engage in 'evidence-based' policy-making, and its determination always and on all issues, no matter what the evidence may show, to be seen as 'tough on crime'. Tens of millions of pounds have been devoted to piloting and evaluating new criminal justice programmes, in the name of evidence-based policy. Preoccupation with media imagery, however, has led to support for harsh, symbolic policies for which there is no supporting evidence, to knee-jerk responses to shocking incidents like the New Year's Eve 2002 gun killings of two young women in Birmingham, and to rhetoric like this from *Justice for All*, a 2002 White Paper: 'The people are sick and tired of a sentencing system that does not make sense' (Home Office 2002a: 86).

Both the tumult and the schizophrenia can be dated from legislative repeal and judicial emasculation of key features of the Criminal Justice Act 1991. That Act, which capped at least five years of careful planning, was not at the time highly controversial, except among judges (Windlesham 1996: 3–10; Dunbar and Langdon 1998: 92–7). Its values were consistent with policies that had reduced the prison population from 50,000 in 1987–88 to 42,500 in 1991.

The 1991 Act had three key features. First, the seriousness of the crime should be the primary determinant of punishment. This expressed retributive, or 'just deserts', ideas about sentencing. The rationales were that punishments in a just system of criminal law should be proportioned to the seriousness of the crime, and that the heavy weight of the research evidence showed that differences in punishments for any given offence have no discernible effects on crime rates. In other words, though many judges believe that the sentences they impose act as deterrents to other would-be criminals, there is no good reason to believe that to be true. Accordingly, there is no good reason why considerations other than those related to just punishments should guide sentencing decisions.

Second, prior criminal convictions should be given relatively little weight in setting sentences. Otherwise, people who had committed a string of minor offences like shoplifting or minor drug sales might be punished more severely than people who committed serious crimes like robbery or rape. That would defy widely shared intuitions about deserved punishments.

Third, convicted people should, whenever possible, be sentenced to community penalties. A new sanction, the unit fine, was created, and the repertoire of other community penalties was reconfigured. The unit fine was a financial penalty meant to be used in place of imprisonment. It could in the number of units ordered be calibrated to the seriousness of the crime, and in the unit's amount (basically the offender's daily net pay) to the offender's financial resources.

The English judiciary quickly, and disingenuously, uncoupled 'proportionality' from just deserts (Windlesham 1996: 20; Faulkner 2001). A key phrase directing that prison sentences be 'commensurate with the seriousness of the offence', the underlying White Paper (Home Office 1990) made clear, was a reference to desert-based ideas about punishment. That White Paper explicitly invoked the scholarly literature on punishment, in which 'just deserts' and 'the proportionality principle' are synonyms, and 'commensurate with the seriousness of the offence' is a term of art.

The Court of Appeal, however, in *Cunningham* (1993) 14 Cr App R (S)

444, redefined the phrase to mean 'commensurate with the punishment and deterrence that the seriousness of the offence requires' (Ashworth 2001: 78). This stood the 1990 White Paper, the 1991 Act, and, since the Parliament can be presumed in enacting government legislation to subscribe to the government's expressed purposes, the will of Parliament, on their heads.

Michael Howard was by then Home Secretary, enthusiastically declaiming that 'Prison works', and enamoured of the apparent successes of 'zero-tolerance policing' in Rudy Giuliani's New York City. The Conservative government in the Criminal Justice Act 1993 quickly abolished unit fines and repealed the legislation directing judges normally to disregard previous convictions in deciding on sentences. It did this largely in reaction to Labour's effort to establish itself as the new tough-on-crime party, exemplified by Tony Blair's slogan, first offered in a 10 January 1993 interview, 'Tough on crime, tough on the causes of crime' (Dunbar and Langdon 1998: 101).

David Downes and Rod Morgan, in their survey of the politics of crime in England and Wales since World War II, described the dynamic:

> First Blair, then Straw, not only dogged Howard's heels; they became his doppelgänger, even his caricature. They beat him to the punch on several fronts. They trumpeted their admiration for the 'zero-tolerance' policing in New York, the need to crack down on 'incivilities', 'squeegie merchants', and beggars. The punitive proposals in the 1994 Criminal Justice and Public Order Bill went unopposed by Labour, as did proposals for mandatory sentencing … Looking back, it is more accurate to see Kenneth Baker and Michael Howard as the prisoners of Blair and Straw's agenda rather than – as generally assumed – the reverse.
>
> (Downes and Morgan 2002: 296–7)

Since then, and particularly since New Labour took office in 1997, criminal justice policy-making in England and Wales has been more theatrical than substantive. Focus groups, tabloid front pages and political advisors have had more influence on government proposals and policies than have criminal justice professionals, systematic evidence or subject-matter experts. Ill-considered but attention-grabbing tough-on-crime proposals – on-the-spot fines for 'louts', housing benefit cuts for truants' parents – are impulsively offered by the Prime Minister or the Home Secretary, and as quickly abandoned. Gun and violence and drug and gangsta rap 'summits' are announced on a week's notice, and generate little except press releases and a few days' headlines. And in 2003, despite dozens of careful evaluations of 'What works?' and solid and insightful policy analyses commissioned by the government, Parliament enacted an omnibus Criminal Justice Act full of misconceived, bound-to-fail and repressive measures. The questions this book addresses are: How could the Labour government have got so much so wrong?, and How, assuming the government really believed its own rhetoric about evidence-based policy, might current policies be refashioned in ways that make them likelier to achieve their nominal goals?

The tumult and schizophrenia continue. The Labour government, and the civil servants it deploys, are of multiple minds. Many people do appear to believe in general in the desirability of evidence-based policy-making. Not everything in the Criminal Justice Act 2003 is single-mindedly repressive or merely politically expedient. Some issues are addressed substantively and on the basis of evidence. Sometimes repressive measures, for example, abrogation of the double-jeopardy doctrine, are so hedged by procedural conditions that they are as much symbolic gestures as law reforms. Sometimes ill-thought-out proposals gradually improved on the path from white paper to bill to act – the community penalties provisions are an example.

A line seems to have been drawn between low-visibility and technical subjects unlikely to attract the attention of the tabloids and high profile, emotive subjects that are. The former are often addressed substantively and on the basis of evidence and experience; the latter symbolically and on the basis of emotion and ideology.

Later chapters discuss particular central law reform subjects and trace out the evolution of key proposals and identify weaknesses and strengths. The first three chapters look in broader terms at the substance and the rhetoric of current and recently proposed crime-control policies. This chapter briefly introduces major recent proposals. Some are evidence-based and sensible. Examples include the creation of a single community punishment order tailored to the offender's risks and needs and placement of greater authority over criminal charges in the hands of the Crown Prosecution Service. Some are muddled and bound to fail to achieve their aims: proposals for a Sentencing Council, sentencing guidelines and suspended sentences are examples. Some lack substance, or sacrifice fundamental human rights of alleged offenders, or both, and are explicable only in terms of populist politics and posturing. Examples include mandatory minimum sentences, preventive detention of 'dangerous offenders', and abrogation of venerable procedures and rules aimed at preventing wrongful convictions.

The second chapter examines the rhetoric and symbolism of English crime-control policy. Why would the recent criminal justice White Paper set 'rebalancing the criminal justice system in favour of the victim' as its primary aim, and what does the phrase mean and the aim imply? Why would the White Paper say the public is 'sick and tired' of a sentencing system 'that does not make sense', and what might those phrases mean? Why would the government feel obliged to respond to every serious crime incident or upward shift in crime rates with 'summits' and ill-considered proposals?

The third chapter ponders the lessons from the first two. The Labour government has apparently decided that an end it values – its own perpetuation in power – justifies undesirable means: adoption of ineffective and mean-spirited crime-control policies. Tony Blair has himself been quoted in the press as acknowledging that his government's proposals for locking up 12- to 15-year-olds in secure facilities are 'horrible', but necessary because the politics of law and order require it (Paveley 2002).

Muddled, poorly informed law reform provisions will fail. They will waste money, damage lives and allow serious problems to continue unabated. Public perceptions of the legitimacy of government and the justice system will be undermined if transparently hypocritical and primarily symbolic policies remain the order of the day. Support for fundamental ideas about liberty will weaken if government consistently abrogates and undermines individuals' protections from the power of the state.

England's Labour Government is in the process of a root-and-branch remaking of the country's criminal justice system. This includes reorganization of criminal justice agencies, setting performance targets and goals, looking for ways to increase cost-effectiveness and efficiency, and altering the statutory framework in numerous ways.

Processes have been under way since 1999 that look toward fundamental changes in the ways criminal courts are organized and operate and in the ways convicted offenders are dealt with. Seven major documents serve as milestones. The first, *The Way Ahead* (Home Office 2001a), is a Labour government policy document published just before the 2001 general election. The second is the final report of the Home Office Review of the Sentencing Framework, *Making Punishments Work* (Home Office 2001b), commonly known as the Halliday report after its head, John Halliday. The third is the report of the Review of the Criminal Courts, commonly called the Auld Report after its author, Sir Robin Auld (Auld 2001). The fourth is a government

White Paper, *Justice for All* (Home Office 2002a), which set out policy proposals partly based on the Auld and Halliday reports. The fifth is the Criminal Justice Bill introduced into Parliament in November 2002. The sixth is the ensuing legislation, the Criminal Justice Act 2003. The seventh, commonly called the Carter Report after its writer Patrick Carter (2003), prepared for the Home Office Strategy Unit, proposes a number of innovations in use of community penalties. It also sets out plans for amalgamating the Probation and Prison Services into a new National Offender Management Service.

Because my emphasis here is mostly on policy proposals relating to punishment of offenders, I devote greatest attention to the Halliday report, the White Paper, and the Criminal Justice Bill and Act. I briefly discuss seven provisions in the Criminal Justice Bill and Act that range from sensible technocratic and substantive ideas through misconceived proposals that are bound to fail, to proposals that can be understood only as symbolic gestures or as cynical efforts to play on public fears and anxieties. For each, I take seriously the idea of evidence-based policy and ask what the evidence is and whether the proposals take it into account.

A number of proposals take the idea of evidence seriously. Not all systematic evidence, however, comes from empirical research. Much comes from professional experience and simple observation. I discuss proposals in a sequence that begins with the sensible and technocratic and ends with the primarily polemical.

Charging

The White Paper and the Bill proposed various ways in which police and prosecutors can work together more efficiently. In particular, they propose that for most significant crimes the power to charge suspects be shifted from the police to the prosecutor (Home Office 2002a, chap. 3). The Act, in sections 28 and 29 and Schedule 2, adopts those proposals. In general, police will make initial decisions as to whether suspects will be charged, released without charge, or referred to prosecutors for a charging decision, but subject to guidance issued by the Director of Public Prosecutions.

These are sensible, experienced-based incremental steps in a long-term shift from use of police prosecutors to use of independent prosecutors. The Crown Prosecution Service is a recent invention. Previously police filed charges, prosecuted lesser cases, and referred serious cases to outside counsel. After the Crown Prosecution Service was established in 1986, police continued to file charges, with inevitable tensions when prosecutors dismissed charges police had filed, claimed that charges were insufficiently grounded in evidence, or otherwise criticized police work.

No doubt police and prosecutors will always complain about each other but it is hard to doubt that shifting authority over charges to the agency that prosecutes them will be more effective and consistent than splitting authority over prosecutions. This is not exciting stuff, and the evidence is mostly experiential, but it counts as sensible, evidence-based policy-making.

Community punishment orders

So do proposals for a single community punishment order to which conditions meeting the circumstances of particular crimes and criminals can be attached. Halliday proposed the creation of a simple penal system consisting of four broad kinds of sanctions: confinement, community/confinement hybrids, community punishment orders and financial penalties. He did this to tidy up confused and complicated prior arrangements, and to allow judges and magistrates more accurately to tailor sentences to offenders' circumstances.

When Halliday wrote in 2001, English sentencers chose from a menu of community penalties that included curfew orders, probation orders, community service orders, combination orders, drug treatment and testing orders, attendance centre orders, exclusion orders and drug abstinence orders. Each had its own governing statutory language and its own technical provisions. The proliferation, said Halliday, was 'not helpful to understanding sentencing. The present law … is complex and should be simplified and made more understandable' (Home Office 2001b: 38). His solution was the creation of a single community punishment order that could encompass any from among a wide range of supervision, treatment, training, work, reparation, residential and other conditions.

Halliday, however, had another main reason for his proposal: the growing and increasingly credible body of evidence on the effectiveness of treatment programmes. The research literature shows, Halliday said, 'some things can work for some people, provided the right programmes are selected and implemented properly' (Home Office 2001b: 7). Further, 'if the programmes are developed and applied as intended, and to the maximum extent possible, reconviction rates might be reduced by 5–15 percentage points (i.e., from the present level of 56 per cent to (perhaps) 40 per cent)'. Halliday also took note of the work of the Joint Accreditation Panel that weighs evidence of crime-reductive effectiveness and classifies and accredits programmes on the basis of the evidence.

Reasonable people can differ about the community punishment order proposal. A system of 'smorgasbord sentencing', in which judges can impose any conditions they like, might result in piling on of conditions that taken in aggregate are much too burdensome or restrictive relative to the seriousness of the offence (Halliday tried to address this by creating three tiers of offences punishable by community penalties, with limitations on available conditions). The proposal might also be accused of making heroic assumptions about capacity for delivering effective programmes. Rigorously evaluated programmes shown to be effective are difficult to replicate. Even when programmes have been successfully replicated, it has proven difficult to impossible to implement them effectively on a large scale (US Surgeon General 2001: chap. 5).

The critiques raise important issues. The key points, however, are that Halliday offered a proposal based on an informed understanding of existing practice and of the evaluative literature on correctional treatment programmes, and that the government adopted it and carried it forward in the White Paper (renamed a 'customised community sentence'; Home Office 2002a: 91) and the Criminal Justice Bill. The Criminal Justice Act 2003 in section 177 established a single 'community order' along Halliday's broad, inclusive lines; and, in section 148, again as Halliday proposed, required that 'the restrictions on liberty imposed' by a community order 'must be such as in the opinion of the court are commensurate with the seriousness of the offence ...'. This is another example of evidence-based policy.

The next two examples are of proposals that were partly evidence-based as they were proposed by Halliday but have been altered by government in ways that make them sure to fail.

Custody plus and minus

Recognizing that the seriousness of some minor crimes, or the punitive attitudes of some magistrates, would inevitably result in imposition of short confinement sentences, Halliday proposed a hybrid 'custody-plus' sentence that would combine confinement with, in effect, a community punishment order. The custody part would be limited to no more than three months. For regular prison sentences, the minimum term would be 12 months, with automatic release, subject to conditions, at the halfway point. Combined, the custody-plus and regular imprisonment proposals would eliminate prison sentences between three and six months.

The government adopted the custody-plus recommendation, and the White Paper, the Bill and the Act all provide for it. Section 181 provides that sentences under 12 months for a single offence may not include more than 13 weeks' confinement and must include at least 26 weeks' release on licence subject to the range of conditions that is available for a community order. Custody-plus thus builds on the proposal for a single community punishment order and rests on the same credible evidentiary base. So far, so good.

But the White Paper also proposed the creation of 'custody-minus' sentences, and here the evidence base falls apart. Custody-minus sentences would be a form of suspended prison sentence, and the full range of conditions possible in any other community sentence would be available. Conditions could be changed if the offender were doing especially well or poorly, but 'any breach will lead to immediate imprisonment' (Home Office 2002a: 93; the point is repeated on pp. 91 and 94). The goal is to reduce prison crowding by diverting offenders who theretofore received prison sentences into community sentences. Nearly everything we know about community penalties and sentencing of minor offenders instructs that custody-minus sentences will fail to achieve that goal.

There are serious problems here (Roberts and Smith 2003). Many offenders, probably a substantial majority, violate conditions. In 1999, official breach rates for probation, community service orders and combination orders were 18, 30, and 29 per cent respectively (Home Office 2001b: app. 6), and those were only the violations of conditions that were noticed and acted upon. People who receive such sentences are usually minor offenders. Taken together, people receiving those three sentences experience 56 per cent reconviction rates within two years from beginning their community penalties. Among released prisoners, those serving short prison terms have higher reconviction rates (60 per cent within two years for those serving a year or less) than those serving longer sentences (28 per cent for those sentenced to four or more years).

Those are *reconviction rates*. Many more minor crimes and violations of conditions will have occurred that passed unnoticed by the authorities, or were noticed but deemed insufficiently important to warrant action, or were acted upon informally, or were acted on formally by means of criminal charges but had not been resolved when the two-year limit tolled.

There are therefore good, practical reasons to doubt that the White Paper's custody-minus proposal for 'immediate imprisonment' following any breach will work. A substantial majority of people sentenced to custody-minus are likely to violate conditions; automatic imprisonment of all of them will increase, not decrease, the prison population. The Bill and Act, though they somewhat weaken the immediate imprisonment policy, create a suspended sentence provision with most of the infirmities of custody-minus.

Parallelling the custody-plus provisions of section 181, section 189 of the Act authorizes imposition of prison sentences for a single offence up to 51 weeks that may be completely suspended and replaced by up to two years' supervision, subject to the same range of possible conditions as characterize custody-plus.[1] Whenever an offender violates 'any of the community requirements [no matter how trivial] of a suspended sentence', the breach conditions in the Act's schedule 12 require a probation officer either to give an official warning or to refer the matter to a court. Once the matter is referred to court, there is a strong statutory presumption that the offender will be sent to prison.[2] Though the Act's suspended sentence provision is less mechanical than the White Paper's custody-minus proposal, it is subject to all the same problems.

A very large percentage of people sentenced to suspended sentences, certainly a majority, will commit the kinds of violations of conditions that under the White Paper would trigger 'immediate imprisonment'. The NEW-ADAM programme showed that 65 per cent of arrestees in 1999–2000 tested positive for heroin or cocaine (Bennett *et al.* 2001). Drug dependence is a chronic, relapsing condition, and most offenders receiving a no-drug-use condition will fail at least once (Hough and Mitchell 2003). A large percentage of offenders will fail to appear for community service, work, or training; violate electronic tagging rules; or commit other non-criminal technical breaches. And, as data summarized a few paragraphs above demonstrate, well over half will be reconvicted within two years.

There are other problems. First, everything we know about creation of 'new' community-based penalties meant to serve as prison alternatives – which the suspended sentence is – tells us that judges at least as often as not use the new penalty for offenders who would otherwise have received something lesser (Petersilia and Turner 1993). This is commonly referred to as 'net-widening' in the sense that the judge casts the community sentence net across a wider range of minor offenders. Net-widening is likely to occur in two ways under the Act's new sentencing provisions. Because the custody-plus sentence allows all the community conditions of a community punishment order, magistrates are likely to use it to give minor offenders a taste of imprisonment before serving their community penalties. However, since custody-plus sentences will eliminate real-time prison sentences between three and six months,[3] judges inclined to impose something longer than three months can impose a suspended sentence of 51 weeks, knowing that breached offenders can be required to serve longer than three months (this may seem an ornate hypothesis, but there is evidence in US jurisdictions of judges doing such things in adapting to new community penalties; Morris and Tonry 1990: chap. 7).

Second, programmes involving closer supervision than theretofore, and intensive supervision programmes generally, which suspended prison sentences often will be, seldom result in higher rates of breach for new crimes but typically result in higher rates of breach for technical violations.

When these two robust findings are combined, creation of a new prison alternative often results in higher overall rates of imprisonment (through the ratcheting-up effects of net-widening combined with higher breach rates; those genuinely diverted from prison will have their normal high failure rate).

The suspended sentence with a strong presumption of immediate imprisonment for every breach thus fails to satisfy the evidence-based policy criterion on three grounds: it takes no account of predictable high rates of failure to comply with conditions, of foreseeable net-widening, and of higher rates of technical breaches associated with intensive supervision. Suspended sentences are unlikely to achieve their purpose of reducing use of imprisonment.

The only thing that will prevent the suspended sentence from backfiring will be wilful circumvention of the breach rules in the Act's schedule 12 by probation officers and magistrates. If probation officers choose to ignore many violations or to respond to them informally, or if magistrates and judges routinely decide that imprisonment would be unjust 'in view of all the circumstances', rather than act on the strong presumption of imprisonment, the suspended sentence may not operate as I have predicted.

The custody-minus/suspended sentence provisions are the first among those I've discussed that cannot be said to be evidence-based. All the evidence points toward the suspended sentence's likely failure to achieve its primary goal of diverting offenders from imprisonment. If predictable net-widening and high breach rates occur, the suspended sentence is likelier to increase than to decrease demand for prison beds.

Here, I believe, is the explanation. At various times during his term as Home Secretary, David Blunkett has purported to want to reduce the prison population and to reduce the use of prison sentences. Halliday's and the Act's custody-plus, by limiting short prison terms to at most 13 weeks and eliminating 13- to 26-week terms altogether, are likely to do that. Encouraging suspension of longer sentences also could do that.

In the White Paper, however, as its polemic showed, the government felt obliged to sound tough. To protect itself from tabloid charges of leniency in its suspended sentence proposals, it promised immediate imprisonment for breach in every case, however little sense that made in policy terms. The Act backs off a bit from that position, but not far. The government was trapped by its own rhetoric and created a new sentence that is unlikely to work.

The evidence doesn't justify either the initial custody-minus proposals or the enacted suspended sentence provisions. Ignorance of the evidence isn't credible. Senior Home Office research and policy specialists know better. Ideology and political self-interest, a wish to appear tough before the media and the public, is what's left.

Sentencing Guidelines Council

Halliday insisted, as an essential component of his comprehensive proposals, 'that new guidelines for the use of judicial discretion will be an essential part of the new framework' (Home Office 2001b: viii). Because his proposals would radically change English sentencing policies, processes and practices, Halliday insisted that sentencing guidelines would be necessary to assure consistent application of the new system and avoid gross disparities in treatment. The Criminal Justice Act 2003, in creating a set of sentencing choices consisting of community orders, custody-plus, intermittent custody, suspended sentences, prison sentences and fines, has enacted just about as radical if less well-considered changes as Halliday proposed.

Halliday's guidelines were to be comprehensive, covering all offences in all magistrates' and higher courts, and very detailed, including criteria for community penalties and for taking account of prior convictions. They would be orders of magnitude more comprehensive and detailed than existing guideline judgements issued by the Court of Appeal or existing non-binding guidelines for magistrates' courts. They were to be developed by an 'independent body', a body to be chaired by the Lord Chief Justice, composed entirely of judges and magistrates, and appointed by the Lord

Chancellor (Home Office 2001b: 55–7). The Act broadly follows the White Paper's proposals except that the Sentencing Council would include a police officer, a prosecutor, a defence lawyer and a victims' advocate among its 12 members. The rest are to be the Chief Justice and seven other judicial members.

A mountain of evidence on sentencing guidelines and sentencing councils gives grounds for predicting that the sentencing guidelines envisaged by the White Paper and the Act will fail. First, councils composed primarily of judges invariably fail to produce meaningful guidelines. Second, the White Paper effectively abandons Halliday's call for comprehensive guidelines and envisages no more than incremental changes to the existing guideline judgements issued by the Court of Appeal. Third, the scheme envisioned by the Act, with a primary role for the Sentencing Council, and lesser roles for the existing Sentencing Advisory Panel and the Home Secretary, is too complex.

Judge-dominated commissions

The ample American experience with sentencing councils (called commissions in the United States) demonstrates that councils composed solely or primarily of judges almost always fail. Partly this is because judges are not policy-makers and are unaccustomed to participation in quasi-legislative rule-making (which is what guideline drafting is). Mostly, however, it is because judges typically oppose meaningful guidelines in principle, believing strongly that judges should be given wide discretion in setting sentences. Judges are less likely than others to believe that current sentences are arbitrary, inconsistent, inappropriate, or otherwise in need of improvement.

Judges are typically happy with the status quo. Recent but telling evidence can be found in the summary of comments sought out by Hilary Benn, MP, as part of a Home Office Review of Correctional Services. One generally held view, Benn reported, is that 'short sentences are particularly ineffective' (Benn 2003: 7). Halliday and the White Paper both said similar things. They are too short to serve rehabilitative or incapacitative ends, but long enough to damage offenders and their families.

One might reasonably expect another widely held, related view that Benn reported: 'Almost all respondents felt there is currently an overemphasis on the use of custody' (p. 7). However, Benn qualified this by noting, 'some sentencers argued that the current balance is right'. Benn concluded, 'It is striking that while most of those observing the sentencers feel that too much use is being made of custody, the sentencers themselves support the current balance between custodial and non-custodial penalties' (p. 8).

A Prison Reform Trust report, which elicited views of 80 magistrates and 48 judges (17 Crown Court, 12 recorders, 14 district judges, 5 senior judges) confirmed Benn's finding. Despite evidence that sentences became much more severe between 1991 and 2001, 'The overall message from the sentencers who took part in this study was that they already use custody sparingly ... it is no surprise that many of the sentencers were resistant to the idea that they should reduce their use of custody' (Hough, Jacobson and Millie 2003: 38–39).

Ian Dunbar and Andrew Langdon (1998: 59), sometime Directors of Inmate Administration and Operational Policy in the Prison Service, describe this as a pervasive problem:

> [F]or 40 years or more, it has not been possible to align sentencing policy with the capacity of the penal system in any way that the judiciary will accept. In crude terms, the courts have usually overfilled whatever prison capacity has been available, and whenever new types of non-custodial penalties have been provided to relieve pressure on the prisons, they have largely been used to punish people who would previously have received a more lenient disposal.

Sentencing councils composed solely or mostly of judges have always failed in the US in one of two ways: either they have been unable or unwilling to develop guidelines and have abandoned the effort, or they have developed guidelines so broad and imprecise that they offered no meaningful constraints to judicial discretion. An English council dominated by judges is highly unlikely to do better. The not-unrepresentative judicial attitudes Benn summarizes help explain why.

The Act gives the judge-dominated council sole authority over the content of guidelines. Proposed guidelines need not be placed before or approved by Parliament. No one need be consulted about draft guidelines except the Home Secretary, such persons as the Lord Chancellor directs, and such other persons 'as the Council considers appropriate'. The council must notify the Sentencing Advisory Panel when it decides to frame or revise guidelines, but not if the council decides 'that the urgency of the case makes it impracticable'. In other words, the Act leaves sentencing policy solely in the hands of the judiciary.

Comprehensiveness

Halliday made it clear that the guidelines must be comprehensive and apply to all courts, if the rest of the proposed radical overhaul was to work. The White Paper played lip service to this, proposing '... a consistent set of guidelines that cover all offences and should be applied whenever a sentence is passed' (Home Office 2002a: 89). Elsewhere, the White Paper made it clear that the process envisaged was one of incremental additions to the body of existing guideline judgements issued by the Court of Appeal, with 'individual guidelines being issued to judges and magistrates ... as and when they are completed' (Home Office 2002a: 90).

It is possible, though unlikely, that the Home Office does not appreciate the significance of the Act's provisions. An 'A-Z: Content of the Bill' document on the Home Office homepage explains that the Sentencing Council will aim to produce a 'robust and comprehensive set of guidelines for all courts'. David Blunkett, likewise, in January 2004, in setting out plans for reorganizing the Prison and Probation Services, asserted that the council, 'will over time formulate a *comprehensive* set of guidelines' (2004: 13; emphasis added).

The Act continues the White Paper's impoverished conception of the nature and functions of a sentencing council. Sentencing guidelines are to be whatever the judge-dominated council wants them to be. They 'may be general in nature or limited to a particular category of offence or offender' (section 170[1]). The council 'may from time to time consider whether to frame sentencing guidelines' (section 170[3]) and when it has prepared draft guidelines must publish them and consult the Home Secretary and such other persons as the Lord Chancellor or the Council itself consider appropriate (section 170[8]).

An argument might be made that the Act contemplates comprehensive guidelines, but by stealth. Because the government could not or would not confront judicial opposition to guidelines, the Act defers to the judiciary but may in its interstices allow space for the government to pressure the council to be more ambitious. Section 170(3) requires the council to 'consider whether to frame' guidelines in respect of particular categories of offences and offenders proposed by the Sentencing Advisory Panel or the Home Secretary. The council is directed by other provisions to consult the Secretary of State and the Sentencing Advisory Panel about draft guidelines and in making decisions, to 'have regard' for the panel's expressed views.

The provisions just cited don't create much room for outside influence on drafting guidelines, but in theory a sufficiently determined

Home Secretary working with a sufficiently determined Sentencing Advisory Panel might be able to assert sufficient pressure to move the council to adopt comprehensive guidelines, but this seems unlikely.

It cannot be coincidence that the judicial members of the Sentencing Council are selected by the Lord Chancellor, that the Home Secretary is to consult senior judges before appointing the non-judicial members, and that the Home Secretary and the Sentencing Advisory Panel are limited to proposing guidelines only for particular categories of offences or offenders. Sympathizers with the judiciary have seen to it that the Act as drafted protects the judiciary's control over sentencing, not only, properly, in individual cases, but also improperly, in relation to sentencing policy generally. There will be no comprehensive guidelines unless the council of its own initiative decides to develop them.

Neither Halliday's nor the government's goals for sentencing guidelines can possibly be achieved unless the guidelines adopted are comprehensive. Comprehensive guidelines cannot be drafted piecemeal, for example, by taking existing Court of Appeal guideline judgements and building around them. Gross anomalies inevitably arise. Another much more important reason it can't work this way is that drafting comprehensive guidelines necessarily entails policy trade-offs. If longer sentences for sex crimes are wanted, for example, then sentences for something else must be shortened. Looking at the sentencing system, and sentences, as a whole is an inherent part of drafting comprehensive guidelines.

Organizational complexity

The organizational scheme envisioned is too complex.[4] The White Paper envisioned that the Sentencing Council would develop guidelines for all courts and all cases. The Act abandoned that goal, except and unless the council of its own initiative adopts it. Even the ability of the Home Secretary and the Sentencing Advisory Panel to require the council to 'consider whether to frame' guidelines, is limited to 'a particular category' of offences or offenders.

The Act, moreover, creates a division of functions of dizzying complexity among the council, the existing Sentencing Advisory Panel, the Court of Appeal and the government. The Sentencing Advisory Panel will 'communicate its views' to the Council. No mention is made in the Act of the existing and future guidelines judgements issued by the Court of Appeal, but comments in the White Paper suggest they will continue to exist and that the Sentencing Advisory Panel will continue to offer advice concerning them.

Setting aside Parliament and various interested constituencies, the Act envisions three major bodies, two composed solely or mostly of judges, involved in the policy process. That wasn't necessary. The Sentencing Advisory Panel could have been folded into the new council; Court of Appeal judges could, with others, have been made members; and the council could have been given explicit authority to revise or repeal existing guideline judgements. The key point is that drafting comprehensive guidelines is an enormous and complicated job and a majority of sentencing councils elsewhere have failed. Giving the job to a part-time council composed mostly of judges, which must share functions with two existing bodies, reduces the odds of success to near zero.

Why might the government have proposed the creation of a sentencing council that can't possibly achieve Halliday's purposes, and creation of guidelines that can't possibly serve as the glue that will hold a refashioned punishment system together? The explanation cannot be evidence or ignorance. The most economical hypothesis is that the government wanted neither to be seen to reject so central a recommendation from Halliday's report, nor to take on the judiciary. In other words, the best hypothesis is that the tabloids don't and therefore the government doesn't, much care one way or another about sentencing guidelines and their underlying aims – fairness to offenders and rational management of resources – and therefore doesn't much care how the Sentencing Council will operate or what it will not accomplish.

Mandatory minimum sentences

Mandatory minimum sentences do not achieve their aims and always produce unwanted side-effects of arbitrariness, injustice in individual cases, hypocritical efforts at circumvention and extreme sentencing disparities (between cases in which the mandatory sentence is imposed and comparable cases in which it is circumvented) (Tonry 1996: chap. 4). This is well known and common ground among public officials and scholars who specialize in sentencing.

A government committed to evidence-based policy-making would, in undertaking wholesale reform of sentencing laws, repeal existing laws providing for mandatory minimum sentences. Certainly it would not propose new ones. The Act, however, leaves most existing mandatories in place and in section 287 establishes a new mandatory minimum five-year sentence for most firearms offences.

Halliday defined mandatory minimums as outside his remit, and did not examine the evidence for and against their use. He did point out, however, that 'many contributors to the review have argued against these sentences, on the grounds that they are inherently likely to result in some disproportionately severe sentences' (Home Office 2001b: 15). He also suggested that at some later time, if the sentencing guidelines were in place and working, Parliament might want to reconsider the wisdom of existing mandatory minimums.

The government felt obliged, gratuitously, to emphasize its support for mandatories. In an auxiliary document to the White Paper, the government summarized its reactions to Halliday's and Auld's recommendations. Accurately noting that Halliday suggested no more than a review someday of whether mandatories would still be needed, the document reports 'We believe that the current provisions are satisfactory' (Home Office 2002b: 10).

This is a particularly clear instance of the evidence pointing one way and the government marching decisively in the other. The story is well known of the passage of mandatory minimum legislation for drug crimes, violent crimes and burglary in the final days of the last Conservative government (e.g., Downes and Morgan 2002). Michael Howard's proposals for such laws were widely seen as bows to law-and-order symbolism, as frantic efforts to appeal to what Sir Anthony Bottoms (1995) famously labelled 'populist punitiveness' in the electorate. It was widely (if in retrospect naively) expected that the new Labour government would let them languish, unimplemented. Instead, in his own bow to the same audience, Jack Straw put them into force. Evidence notwithstanding, the current government appears committed to mandatory minimums.

Preventive detention

Policy-makers in every country worry about pathologically violent offenders and horrifying crimes. The profoundly difficult problems, however, are that really serious crimes happily are rare and unhappily are very difficult to predict. About the best that policy-makers can do is to try to devise systems for identifying people who present significant risk of committing serious violent or sexual crimes and then try to monitor or control their behavior.

Halliday proposed creation of a new kind of determinate prison sentence for high-risk people: release would not be automatic when half was served, as with other prison sentences, but would require an individualized decision by the parole board. Halliday cautioned that it should be used 'only when there were *high* risks of re-offending and *serious* harm' (emphases added). Serious harm he defined as death or serious personal injury. He worried that the special sentence might be misused or overused: 'It will be important to set a threshold for this sentence to ensure that it is reserved for dangerous offenders, and not used inappropriately' (Home Office 2001b: 33). And at the end of the sentence, the offender would have to be released. Mental health commitments might be appropriate at that point for those who were seriously mentally disturbed, but the rest would have to be allowed to get on with their lives. Some might someday commit a new serious crime, but the need to balance risk and liberty requires that risks be taken.

The White Paper's proposals for violent and sexual offenders are profoundly anti-civil libertarian and reject all of Halliday's limits and cautions. Instead 'they' would be sentenced to indeterminate sentences and be held 'until their risks are considered manageable in the community'. They would remain in custody 'until the Parole Board was *completely satisfied* that the risk had sufficiently diminished' and the prisoner could then remain on licence for the rest of his or her life (Home Office 2002a: 95; emphasis added). 'Completely satisfied' is a test that could never be met.

Nowhere in the discussion of sentences for violent and sexual offences is there a trace of nuance or subtlety, a suggestion that the proposals involve fundamental trade-offs, or that prospective predictions of dangerousness are devilishly difficult and much more often than not inaccurate (Matravers and Hughes 2003; Monahan 2004).

The Act backs off somewhat from the White Paper's rhetoric and contains provisions resembling Halliday's recommendations, though they are broader and more susceptible to the overuse and misuse Halliday feared.

The overbreadth takes three forms. First, the provisions are triggered by convictions of any of 65 specified violent offences and 88 specified sexual offences, only some of which could possibly count as acts typically committed by dangerous offenders. Some, such as rape and assaults causing grievous bodily harm, are self-evidently serious crimes potentially involving death or serious personal injury. Others, such as kidnapping, which under some circumstances may be no more than an incident of an unhappy divorce proceeding; and manslaughter, which may be the tragic consequence of a routine motor vehicle offence, are only sometimes seriously culpable crimes. Still others, such as intercourse with an animal, voyeurism, exposure, possession of pornographic photographs of children, and solicitation by men, do not inherently involve death or serious injury.

Second, the Act creates a number of presumptions against liberty. Any adult offender who is charged with any of the 153 specified offences, and who was previously convicted of any of them, is assumed to present a serious risk to the public of serious harm (section 229). To avoid imposing a special 'dangerous offender' sentence, a court must find that it would be unreasonable to conclude such a risk exists. Thus, a person previously convicted of achieving sexual congress with a sheep, on doing it again, would be presumed to be dangerous, but to people rather than sheep. Once imprisoned under the dangerous offender provisions, an offender is not, like other prisoners, entitled to automatic release on licence on serving half the sentence, but may be held until it expires. Earlier release is permitted only if the Parole Board 'is satisfied that it is no longer necessary for the protection of the public that the prisoner should be confined' (section 247). Only then may a 'dangerous' offender be released before expiration of the prison sentence.

Third, the basic finding of dangerousness is to be made by a judge, according to vague criteria: 'whether there is a significant risk to members of the public of serious harm [defined as "death or serious personal injury, whether physical or psychological"]' (section 229). Everything we know about predictions of dangerousness instructs that judges tend to overpredict and that judges' individualized predictions are less accurate than are statistical predictions. Note that Halliday would have required a 'high' risk of death or serious physical injury. The Act requires only a 'significant' risk of serious psychological injury (whatever that might be).

Why would Halliday's proposals have been so starkly expanded and his cautions so completely ignored? Here again evidence clearly isn't the answer: there is no evidence that sexual intercourse with sheep threatens serious harm to members of the public. And the cautionary evidence on predictions of dangerousness is well known.

The explanations are self-evident. The government does not much care about civil liberties of offenders and desperately cares that it not be blamed when the next horrifying crimes occur. Sexual offences strike powerful emotional chords in many people. Why, by sensibly distinguishing between those that genuinely threaten serious harm and those that do not, risk having someone, anyone, accuse the government of insufficient vigilance concerning sexual deviance?

Protections against wrongful convictions

The White Paper proposes and the Criminal Justice Act enacts a wide range of changes in how trials are conducted and in related policies (Padfield and Crowley 2003). These include abrogation of the many-centuries-old double-jeopardy rule, elimination of rules forbidding admission of hearsay evidence, allowing admission into evidence of information about offenders' prior offences, and narrowing of jury trial rights.

The reasons for the traditional rules are straightforward. The imbalance in power and resources between the state and any individual is so great, and the stress, anxiety and expense of defending oneself in a trial are so exhausting, that the double-jeopardy rule forbids subjecting any individual to that experience twice. The hearsay rules exist as a protection against inaccurate information and through that against wrongful convictions. The rules against admitting information about prior crimes into evidence aim to increase the likelihood that convictions occur because the evidence proves the defendant committed the crime with which he is charged, rather than, prejudicially, because prior convictions show the defendant to be an unsympathetic or untrustworthy person. Jury trial rights are meant to protect the liberty of citizens and assure that cross-sections of ordinary people agree with the state functionaries who file criminal charges.

The Act eliminates the double-jeopardy rule, greatly narrows the scope of the hearsay rule, permits introduction of evidence of offenders' prior crimes, and narrows jury trial rights.

All of these changes diminish procedural protections and civil liberties in England and Wales and most will increase the prevalence of convictions of innocent people. No empirical evidence is given in the White Paper that the problems any of the proposed changes are meant to address are quantitatively important. That is, no evidence is given to show that significant numbers of guilty people are avoiding convictions because of the existing rules. No doubt some are, but equally there is no doubt that some innocent people are now convicted. At least since the time of Blackstone, wise consensus has existed that wrongful acquittals are a far less worrisome problem than are wrongful convictions. Most of the proposals described in this subsection, if adopted, will increase the number of wrongful convictions. The double-jeopardy rule change will expose acquitted people to retrial because politicians decide it is in their political interest to do so.

What is the reason for these proposals? In the United States, right-wing politicians have insisted for many years that one must be 'for victims' or 'for criminals'. If that choice must be made, few politicians will risk being seen as having thrown in their lot with criminals. Until the early 1990s, English politicians resisted the view that so nonsensical a choice need be made. By pinioning so much of its crime-control policy on the bromide that the criminal justice system must be rebalanced in favour of the victim, the Labour government has in effect declared itself 'for victims'. Anything that is 'against criminals' is by definition in favour of victims. Increasing the odds of wrongful convictions is thus a way to demonstrate sympathy for victims.

The procedural changes seem in some ways more symbolic than substantive. Though the double-jeopardy rule has been repealed, for example, before an acquitted offender may be retried, the Director of Public Prosecutions must authorize re-prosecution, a prosecutor must apply to the Court of Appeal for permission, new and 'compelling' evidence must be available, and the Court of Appeal must decide that re-prosecution is 'in the interests of justice' (sections 75–79). The restrictions of jury trial likewise are slight, allowing only for prosecutions without juries in some complex fraud cases and in cases where there is danger of jury tampering.

The procedural changes seem primarily to be a response to populist and tabloid mythology that procedural protections somehow offer an unfair advantage to criminals, rather than a wholesale attack on civil liberties. They seem more aimed at allowing Labour to *say* it had abolished the double-jeopardy rule than in practice to do it. However, each time the government, in pursuit of tabloid approbation, undermines the principles on which civil liberties rest, it makes their survival more precarious.[5]

* * * *

The seven features of the Criminal Justice Act that I have discussed were not entirely arbitrarily chosen; others could have been selected, but they are among the most substantial and politically contentious of the Act's provisions. They demonstrate an inverse relation between the government's reliance on evidence and the political salience of a subject. In relation to the changed roles of police and prosecutors in formulating criminal charges, and the design of the new community punishment order, evidence has been considered and taken into account. These, however, are technical and intra-institutional issues that provoke little political or public controversy. At the spectrum's other end, in relation to defendants' procedural protections and dangerous offenders – issues about which the tabloids bray – evidence seems neither to have been consulted nor to have played a role.

Where there was no powerful constituency to be faced down, as with changes in the charging rules, evidence mattered. Where a powerful constituency was affronted, as with development of sentencing guidelines, the government backed down.

The Labour government's has been a sorry performance. If the principal drivers of crime-control policy proposals are evidence, ignorance and ideology or self-interest, ideology and self-interest won the day. The next chapter considers how that could have happened.

Footnotes

1 There is a serious tariff problem here. The supervision period for a suspended sentence may according to subsection 189(3) range between 26 and 104 weeks while under section 181 the supervision (licence) period under a custody-plus sentence may range between 26 and 49 weeks. The reasonable inference is that suspended sentences are meant as punishments for more serious offences than are custody-plus sentences and yet custody-plus sentences must include 2–13 weeks' imprisonment and suspended sentences may not include any prison time.

2 By contrast, the Act's schedule 8, setting out procedures for handling violations of conditions of custody-plus orders, accords sentencers broader discretion and neither requires nor presumes imprisonment.

3 This is because the prison component of a custody-plus sentence may not exceed 13 weeks and standard sentences of a year or longer include 50 per cent as a period of automatic release on license. A 12-month nominal sentence includes 6 months in prison.

4 It is just possible, though surprising given the professionalism of Home Office civil servants, that planners have fundamentally misunderstood what is involved in developing meaningful guidelines. The Carter Report indicates that the Sentencing Council 'would need to develop quickly a comprehensive set of guidelines', an unrealistic goal. Elsewhere, Carter indicates that 'each year' the council should discuss 'the priorities for sentencing practice with the Home Office' and 'then issue guidelines' (Carter 2003: 5, 31). Annual changes would quickly discredit the guidelines and prove an administrative nightmare.

5 I may give the government too much credit in these paragraphs. Several readers of a draft of this chapter pointed out that the limited reach of some of the procedural changes results from entrenched opposition in the House of Lords.

Chapter 2

Rhetoric

So why, after so long a gestation and so much serious work, did England's Labour government enact a Criminal Justice Act that contained so many proposals that are half-baked (e.g., the Sentencing Council and sentencing guidelines, suspended sentences), that reject long-standing ideas about fairness (e.g., double-jeopardy, prophylactic rules aimed at minimizing wrongful convictions), or that celebrate symbol over substance (e.g., mandatory minimums, dangerous offenders)?

The answer is neither merely that the government is concerned about public opinion nor that it wants to be re-elected. That's true of all governments, including those that do not trumpet their commitment to evidence-based policy. Public opinion in any case, as ministers know, is much more nuanced, balanced and sensible than are the editorial pages and front-page stories of the *Sun* or the *News of the World*. Home Office research has repeatedly shown that the public is poorly informed and wildly inaccurate in its views. In particular, despite declining crime rates in England and Wales since the mid-1990s, the 2003 British Crime Survey showed that 43 per cent of people who read tabloids thought that the crime rate had increased a lot, nearly twice the percentage of broadsheet readers (Simmons and Dodd 2003: 127). This finding illustrates why it makes little substantive sense to base policy on the views of tabloid editors or readers.

Home Office research has also shown that ordinary people, when asked what sentence they would impose for particular crimes, typically propose sentences less harsh than judges now impose (Hough and Roberts 1998; Home Office 2002b: app. 5). Home Office and other research has repeatedly shown that ordinary people usually consider rehabilitation the most important aim of sentencing (Home Office 2001b: app. 5) and are more willing to see tax monies spent on rehabilitative programmes than on prisons (Roberts *et al.* 2003).

Nor can the answer be ministers' ignorance, naiveté, or inexperience. Sometimes in American, Canadian or Australian state legislatures that have high turnover of citizen legislators, those may be reasons why poorly considered legislation is enacted. They can't credibly be argued to explain policy-making in the English national government. Most MPs are career politicians. English ministers are surrounded by talented and well-informed civil servants and have ready and easy access through them to relevant bodies of systematic knowledge. The Home Office's research, development and statistics department is the largest and most sophisticated agency of its type in the world. And, because 'consultation with stakeholders' is now commonplace, ministers have easy access to the views of practitioners and other interested parties. The Home Office published at least two summaries of views offered during consultations relating to the White Paper's proposals (Home Office 2002b; Benn 2003).

Not much is left once inexperience, ignorance, and naiveté are set aside except ideology and political self-interest. These last are a large part of the answer but so also are deeper grains in contemporary English culture. Whatever the deeper reasons, many recent criminal justice policy developments are better understood, as Chapter 1 showed, as exercises in symbolic politics than as outgrowths of evidence-based policy. In this chapter, I look first at the government's recent rhetoric, then at persistent, almost epiphenomenal, pre-occupations with persistent and dangerous offenders, and finally at what have become widely known as knee-jerk proposals and media-event crime 'summits'. After that, in Chapter 3, I step back to ponder why the Labour government so often in formulation of criminal justice policy prefers rhetoric over substance.

Rhetoric

The Criminal Justice Act 2003 is a work in legislative draftsmanship, and does not explain itself. The best source of explanations is the White Paper that preceded it. The White Paper contains two (among many) rhetorical flourishes that warrant unpacking. The first is the White Paper's 'single clear priority: to balance the criminal justice system in favour of the victim' (Home Office 2002a: 14). The second is an especially florid bit of polemic in the chapter on sentencing that begins: 'The public are sick and tired of a sentencing system that does not make sense' (p. 86).

Balancing the criminal justice system in favour of the victim

Senior police officials of late, including Sir John Stevens, Commissioner of the Metropolitan Police, have frequently expressed similar aims. The language comes straight from the pages of tabloid papers. Lord Windlesham examined crime coverage of the *Sun*, the *Daily Mail*, and the *Times* during August 1993, and interrogated their editors. His summary of newspapers' messages is that:

> The balance in the criminal justice system had been tilted towards the protection of the innocent at the expense of failing to convict the guilty; and too often the interests of the offender (the description 'the criminal' being invariably preferred) were put above those of the victim.
>
> (Windlesham 1996: 48)

What can the undertaking to balance the system more in favour of the victim possibly mean? In some contexts, words like these might be phatic, entirely expressive, not meant to communicate literal meanings. Empathy for victims is the message to be conveyed; the literal meanings of the words are not important. This seems unlikely. Stevens makes his speeches with what looks and sounds like real passion. And the White Paper contains many calls for new programmes for victims and for reduced procedural protections for alleged and convicted offenders.

The meaning must be substantive, but what is it? One claim, implicit in the idea of balance, is that the criminal justice system is a zero-sum game in which everything that benefits offenders hurts victims and vice versa. Or to use a different metaphor: justice is a pie of fixed size; a larger piece for victims means a smaller piece for offenders, and vice versa. A second is that victims suffer psychic harm or personal frustration when alleged offenders are not convicted, or are punished less severely than victims want. A third, explicit, argument is that the system is now somehow 'balanced against' the victim.

On these arguments, reducing procedural protections for offenders, and increasing the prevalence of wrongful convictions, hurts offenders, helps victims, and rebalances the system. None of these claims, however, stands up to analysis.

The idea that the criminal justice system is a zero-sum game, in which every gain for one player is a loss for the other, is wrong. In Western countries, the parties in a criminal prosecution are the state and the defendant. The victim is certainly an interested party, and as a witness may be a necessary participant, but the litigation is not between the victim and the defendant.

This has several important implications. Treating victims well, better, or sympathetically does no damage to the defendant, and I've heard no one suggest that it does. Seen from the offender's perspective there is no zero-sum game. Nothing that is done to help victims need damage offenders.

There are good reasons why the state should be sympathetic to victims' suffering and needs, and should develop programmes to address them, but 'rebalancing the system against offenders' is not one of them. Chapter 2 of the White Paper offers a raft of proposals, many worthy, for improvements in addressing victims' needs. Reasonable people will differ over the details, but few will disagree that victims should be dealt with sympathetically and supportively. That, however, implies nothing about treating defendants and offenders badly.

The reverse implication also is true: treating offenders well, better, or sympathetically does no damage to victims. Victims have the same interests as other citizens in having a criminal justice system that is fair, efficient and humane, and it is hard to see how they benefit from its degradation.

There are good reasons – including personal self-interest – why victims should oppose changes that treat defendants and offenders worse. Research on the prevalence of convictions shows that upwards of 33 per cent of men and 9 per cent of women are convicted for a standard list offence (i.e., excluding traffic and similar offences) at least once by age 46 (McClintock and Avison 1968; Prime *et al.* 2001). Home Office research on self-reported delinquency shows 57 per cent of males and 37 per cent of females aged 12–30 admitted committing at least one serious offence (Flood-Page *et al.* 2000). The Home Office figures are regarded by most experts as underestimates. The Cambridge Study in Delinquent Development, for example, found that 92 per cent of London males admitted committing a serious offence by age 32 (Farrington 2002). Research on victimization shows that offenders have especially high rates of victimization by others and accordingly that victims and offenders are often the same people, repeatedly changing role over time (Stratford and Roth 1999). Many of one day's victims will benefit in future from changes designed to treat defendants better, and, of course, will suffer the effects of changes that treat today's offenders worse.

So the zero-sum game argument is wrong. What about the second claim, that convictions should be made easier to achieve, and punishments be made harsher, because victims will thereby be made happier? This is at heart a proposal that government should knowingly increase the incidence of wrongful convictions in order to make victims happier. That can't be a morally legitimate proposal in a society that subscribes to a political philosophy of individual rights in which respect for the moral autonomy of individuals requires that they be left alone by the state except when their wrongful behaviour justifies intrusion. From that starting point, the state is justified in depriving people of liberty only when and because they have acted in blameworthy ways. If individuals are not morally culpable, they should not be convicted or punished no matter how many victims might thereby be made happy.

An immediate comeback is that there are other morally justifiable starting points, and that utilitarian 'greatest-good-of-the-greatest-number' concerns sometimes justify the sacrifice of individuals. Philosopher Ronald Dworkin (1988) has shown why that proposition is ethically unacceptable in this context. Dworkin was trying to sort out a seeming conflict between equality values and democratic values. The conflict arose over the question whether black applicants to Texas law schools could categorically be denied admission when there were reasons to suspect that a majority of voters supported a policy of racial exclusion. In democratic societies, people are entitled to act from self-interest and to vote according to their preferences. So the question was, if a majority of preferences expressed by Texans favoured exclusion of blacks, wouldn't that justify such a policy?

Dworkin's answer is 'No'. He explained that we must distinguish between personal and external preferences in thinking about policies concerning fundamental interests of citizens. Personal preferences, what we want for ourselves, should always count and be counted. So should positive external preferences, beneficial things we want for others. Negative preferences, however, such as wanting to deny particular educational opportunities to black people, or to cause injury to others, should neither count nor be counted. Thus even if a clear majority of Texans wanted to deny opportunities to blacks, that view is not ethically entitled to prevail.

A similar analysis applies to victims' external preferences that more offenders be convicted, even if that means more wrongful convictions, or that offenders receive harsher sentences than they deserve. Victims' personal preferences for formulation of policies that better meet their needs should count. Their negative external preferences that offenders should be treated unjustly, or unduly severely, should not. This is especially true in relation to current government proposals. The appeals to victims' wants are primarily rhetorical and public opinion research shows that victims and citizens generally badly misunderstand how the justice system works and substantially underestimate the severity of current punishments.

That leaves the third claim, that the system is now somehow balanced against the victim. The White Paper identifies a number of respects in which victims could be treated better. The extent and content of victim services could be improved. So could provision, when needed, of medical care, counselling services and material support. Victims could be treated more solicitously. Systems of setting and changing court dates, and notifying victims and witnesses, could be made more efficient and more convenient. Victims could be provided with more frequent, complete and understandable information. All of those things could be done, and should be, but none of them would damage defendants and offenders. If current procedures and policies treat victims less sympathetically than they should, that's a problem, but it's a problem in its own right, and not one caused by solicitude or procedural protections accorded defendants and offenders.

The White Paper says that 'many victims feel that the rights of offenders take precedence over theirs' (2002a: 37). This may be how some victims characterize their perception that they are not treated well, but that's a confusion. The problem is that their rights and interests do not receive the consideration they think they should, not that offenders are in some way treated better.

So what can the White Paper mean when it says the system needs rebalancing in favour of victims? If it means only that some procedures and processes can be made more effective or efficient, that may be true, but it has nothing to do with rebalancing. If it means that procedures should be changed to produce more convictions, that may or may not be true, but again it's nothing to do with rebalancing. It may mean, and probably does mean, that victims and the rest of us resent and dislike offenders and that the government wishes to manipulate those emotions so that we will think it tough on crime. That has nothing to do with rebalancing, and it is ignoble.

The public are sick and tired ...

Three connected statements frame the White Paper chapter that proposes a root-and-branch overhaul of English sentencing laws and practices:

> [1] The public are sick and tired of a sentencing system that does not make sense. [2] They read about ... serious offenders who get off lightly, or are not in prison long enough or for the length of their sentence ... [3] The system is so muddled that the public do not always understand it.
>
> (Home Office 2002a: 86)

This is polemic of a sort not commonly found in White Papers or other serious policy documents. The first proposition is empty. Nowhere does the White Paper say why or in what ways the public believes sentencing 'does not make sense'. In most ways the English system of processing criminal cases closely resembles those of every Western country – the same kinds of functionaries, procedures, criminal laws, punishment options. Processing contested cases takes time; the rules are technical; sometimes innocent people are convicted or guilty people go free. If the English system doesn't make sense, nor does that of any country.

The second proposition consists of generalizations that lead nowhere. Who is to say that any particular offender got off lightly or – the same thing – was not in prison long enough? Reasonable people differ in such opinions, but, more importantly for policy purposes, we know that lay people significantly underestimate the severity of punishments imposed and themselves favour punishments less severe than are now used (Hough and Roberts 1998). Finally, that prisoners are not in prison for the full announced lengths of their sentences is simply a description of the current English sentencing system. It is also a description of the sentencing system proposed in the White Paper and contemplated in the Criminal Justice Act 2003, in which most prisoners will be released after serving half their sentence. If the public was outraged or wilfully deceived by English laws before the Act was passed, they will be outraged and wilfully deceived by the system the Act will put in its place.

The third proposition also leads nowhere. That the sentencing system is complicated and that people do not 'always understand' it goes without saying. Better public education programmes might help people understand it somewhat better and no doubt it could be tweaked in various ways to make it slightly simpler. The reality, though, is that the sentencing system, like the environmental protection, sanitation and health-care systems, is complicated. Participants who work in it day by day understand things that casual observers will not.

This bit of rhetoric, like the rebalancing-the-system rhetoric, does not survive deconstruction.

Substance

A number of themes have characterized Labour government policy pronouncements and preoccupations since at least 1993, and they exhibit the same tensions between symbol and substance as does its rhetoric. Two examples are the focus on 'persistent' and 'dangerous' offenders. Both are legitimate subjects of policy concern and there is no reason to doubt that current policies and practices could be improved to deal more effectively with them. The ways in which the government proposes to deal with them, however, ignore empirical evidence, practical experience and civil liberties issues that most informed people consider relevant or decisive.

Persistent offenders

'Persistent' minor offenders have long had totemic significance for New Labour. The Criminal Justice Act 1991, premised on the just-deserts idea that the offender's current crime should be the primary determinant of his sentence, aimed at 'diverting from custody those petty, persistent offenders jailed more for their persistence than for the seriousness of their crimes'. By early 1993, Labour was hammering away, attacking 'the key provisions of the 1991 Criminal Justice Act – the emphasis on just deserts for the current offence rather than for previous convictions' and accusing the Tories of 'undue leniency in sentencing' (Downes and Morgan 2002: 295).

Labour was not alone in this:

> By the early Spring of 1993 ... a number of countervailing forces were gaining ground rapidly ... [t]he police led a sophisticated campaign on the issue of persistent juvenile offenders, quickly converted by the media into a moral panic, and prompting a new home secretary, Kenneth Baker, to announce that 'secure training centres' would be provided to hold children as young as 12 years.
> (Rutherford 1996: 127)

In a paper prepared in Spring 1996 for the Parliamentary Labour Party, Jack Straw argued that sentencing 'should give particular attention to the sentencing of repeat offenders to ensure that proper account is taken of progression in sentencing' (quoted in Dunbar and Langdon 1998: 125). Labour's 1997 election manifesto undertook to get tough with them, the antisocial behaviour orders created by the Crime and Disorder Act 1998 were aimed at them, and each major crime-control document of the twenty-first century gives them focal attention.

The pre-election policy document, *Criminal Justice: The Way Ahead,* pledged to 'get to grips with the 100,000 most persistent criminals' and to assure that punishments become 'progressively more intense for persistent offenders' (Home Office 2001a: 8, 20). Halliday's charge from Jack Straw, the Home Secretary, made clear that handling persistent offenders should be a priority. Perhaps not surprisingly, of the 'most compelling' problems to be addressed, the first that Halliday listed is 'the unclear and unpredictable approach to persistent offenders' and among his major proposals is that 'there should be a new presumption that severity of sentence will increase as a result of recent and relevant previous convictions' (Home Office 2001b: ii, v). The White Paper followed suit (2002a: 88).

So does the Criminal Justice Act 2003. Section 143, a general section on determining the seriousness of an offence, provides that the court 'must treat each previous conviction as an aggravating factor ...'. In section 153(2) on lengths of custodial sentences, the length is to be 'commensurate with the seriousness of the offence, or the combination of the offence and one or more offences associated with it'. The last phrase recurs in several other sections.

As a person who has been interested in crime-control policy for a third of century, but who came to England only in 1999, I find this all a bit bewildering. Nuisance offenders exist everywhere, but only in England have they become a major and chronic policy preoccupation. Persistent perpetrators of minor, mostly property and drug, crimes exist in every city, in every land, in every time. Many are young, and most grow out of it. Many are drug users, and have a hard time breaking free of crime until they've broken their dependence on drugs. Some are mentally handicapped and beset by a wide range of personal, family and economic problems. Most are unemployed and some are homeless.

They are a foreseeable element of life in modern Western cities. They present dilemmas to police, prosecutors, judges and the community. The crimes they commit are typically minor – shoplifting, petty theft, drug sales, public drunkenness – and they commit them at staggering rates. A man who has been arrested eight times, for example, has an 87 per cent likelihood (86 per cent for women) of a ninth arrest (Prime *et al.* 2001), but the offences are often so minor that anything more than a minor community penalty or a very short prison sentence would be unjustly and disproportionately harsh.

Judges find these cases perplexing. An experienced and thoughtful English judge has examined the challenges that such offenders present in detail (Jones 2002). The offences they commit, though minor relative to more serious crimes, are often not minor to the victims. In aggregate, minor property crimes are a serious social problem. The difficulty, Jones writes, is in knowing what to do. A two- or three-month prison sentence might be justifiable in light of an offender's current and past crimes, but the judge who imposes it seldom expects it to accomplish anything useful. He knows that the risk factors associated with those crimes will not go away. If the offender is an active drug user, has no permanent residence, no job, no job skills and no income, his situation will be exactly the same when he exits prison as when he enters. Probably there are few or no community programmes to give the offender the support and structure he needs, and if there are he's unlikely to do well in them. So the judge knows that almost anything he or she does is likely to be fruitless. Yet locking such a person up for life or a term of years would be profoundly unjust. What to do? Responsible judges do the best their intuition allows, and hope that such people will age out of this period of their lives. Most do.

The recurring Labour government proposal is that such people receive an additional increment of punishment for each conviction. For a homely example, if a third shoplifting merited a three-month sentence, the fourth might warrant five months, the fifth seven months, and so on. This is a proposal that makes little policy sense. Imprisoning huge numbers of minor offenders is enormously expensive but offers no realistic prospects of deterring that offender or anyone else. Nor does it offer any meaningful prospect of rehabilitating him. Some minor crimes might be prevented through the offender's incapacitation, but how many would have to be prevented to cost-justify £35,939 per year per prisoner in confinement costs (Home Office 2003)? And minor crimes, no matter how many, cannot justify imposition of lengthy prison sentences.

Is there nothing policy-makers can do? Of course there is, as a recent report from the government's Social Exclusion Unit (Social Exclusion Unit 2002) explains. A wide range of social, educational and treatment programmes can be targeted on young persistent offenders. Creative diversion programmes can be developed and restorative justice programmes be expanded. Judges can impose appropriate minor punishments so that actions have consequences and basic social values are upheld. Sentencing guidelines can specify what those sentences should normally be. But the temperature should be lowered and youth workers, probation officers and judges allowed to get on with their efforts to ameliorate this chronic but inevitable social problem.

There is an apparent, but unfounded, logic to the proposal that each successive offence receive a harsher punishment – deterrence. If offenders are threatened with a harsher penalty if they do it again, surely they won't. Many, though by no means all, judges appear to believe that the sentences they impose in individual cases will deter other would-be wrongdoers. On the face of it, that logic makes sense.

The only, but overwhelming, problem with this logic is that there is no evidence that it works. Every serious review of research on the deterrent effects of punishment has concluded that there is no evidence to support the belief that incremental changes or differences in punishments in individual cases, or in general, have measurable deterrent effects.

A recent report on the subject commissioned by the Home Office so found (von Hirsch *et al.* 1999). So have a series of reports commissioned from the US National Academy of Sciences by Republican Presidents Gerald Ford and Ronald Reagan (Blumstein *et al.* 1978; Reiss and Roth 1993) and every authoritative review of the literature in the last quarter century (e.g., Cook 1980; Nagin 1998; Doob and Webster 2003).

Most people who deal with persistent minor offenders know this. Here's how the White Paper that underlay the Criminal Justice Act 1991 explained it:

> Deterrence is a principle with much immediate appeal. Most law abiding citizens ... would be deterred by the shame of a criminal conviction or the possibility of a severe penalty. There are doubtless some criminals who carefully calculate the possible gains and risks. But much crime is committed on impulse, given the opportunity presented by an open window or an unlocked door, and it is committed by offenders who live from moment to moment; their crimes are as impulsive as the rest of their feckless, sad or pathetic lives. It is unrealistic to construct sentencing arrangements on the assumption that most offenders will weigh up the possibilities in advance and base their conduct on rational calculation.
>
> (Home Office 1990: 6)

Lest it be thought that the state of the evidence has changed since that 1990 White Paper was written, consider what John Halliday had to say:

> [T]here seems to be no link between marginal changes in punishment levels and changes in crime rates … It is the prospect of getting caught that has deterrence value, rather than alterations to the 'going rate' for severity of sentences … The evidence suggests that any new sentencing framework should make no new assumptions about deterrence.
>
> (Home Office 2001b: 8–9)

So there really is no evidence on which to base claims that incrementally harsher punishments for each offence committed by a persistent offender will affect crime rates. The Carter Report, a product of the Home Office Strategy Unit, explicitly reaches the same conclusion: 'There is no evidence that, say, a 15 month sentence is any less effective than a 18 month sentence in terms of reducing re-offending' (Carter 2003: 30).

Why then do persistent minor offenders so preoccupy the Labour government? Two hypotheses come to mind. The first is that this government is unusually authoritarian, as illustrated by frequent accusations of control-freakery and centralization of all serious decision-making and authority in the Cabinet Office and the central government. Offenders who persist in their behaviour are behaving defiantly when they disregard a 'Do it again and ...' threat, and this government doesn't deal well with defiance.

This may be a demonstration of the effects of what Downes and Morgan (2002) call Margaret Thatcher's successful effort in the 1980s to equate deviance, of the sort criminals engage in, with defiance, of the sort demonstrators and striking workers engage in. Thatcher, they say, successfully conflated the two and thereby de-legitimated strikes and demonstrations; in effect she redefined defiance as deviance. Before that, strikes and other efforts by organized labour to assert the interests of workers were often defiant but were generally seen as legitimate, as today they are in France, even if often they are inconvenient, frustrating, unruly and confrontational.

Mrs Thatcher's government effectively de-legitimated the miners' strikes and the miners themselves, who were, after all, doing no more than unions and workers have always tried to do – protect jobs and the interests of workers and their families.

The conflation of defiance with deviance has worked backwards for the Labour government. Minor crimes and nuisance offenders are irritating and frustrating. There is no question they can be characterized as deviance and deviants. The government, however, seems to see deviance as defiance, something it is not prepared to countenance. The latest shoplifting or drug sale or non-criminal antisocial behaviour is bad in its own right but additionally bad because it defies the authority of the state and the values of right-thinking people. This is the logic behind the government's antisocial behaviour orders: that defiance of a civil court order concerning non-criminal behaviour can justify, and result in, a criminal conviction.

The second hypothesis is that the government is simply cynical and politically self-interested. Persistent offenders are a nuisance, and an easy target for stereotyping. They can easily be combined with 'yobs', 'louts', and 'neighbours from Hell' into a vulnerable and politically powerless symbol of categories of people who make other people worried and unhappy. They are also generally not the children of the middle and upper classes, which means that they can easily be stereotyped in voters' minds, much as Republican politicians in the United States successfully stereotyped underclass black offenders and drug dealers in American voters' minds. No other political party in England will stand up for persistent offenders. The hypothesis then is that toughness on persistent offenders is simply part of the Labour government's tough-on-crime script and they see no reason to move away from it. Put more directly, the preoccupation with persistent offenders may have little if anything to do with persistent offenders and everything to do with image-positioning.

Dangerous offenders

Proposals for dealing with dangerous offenders are touched on in Chapter 1 and discussed at some length in Chapter 6, so I mention them but briefly here.

It is striking that the government's policy proposals concerning dangerous offenders became increasingly more repressive with the passage of time. *Criminal Justice: The Way Ahead*, the April 2001 pre-election policy document, set out a balanced and restrained approach to dealing with 'dangerous offenders'. For starters, it narrowly restricted the group of offenders targeted to 'individuals who are dangerous and suffer from a severe personality disorder' or who 'pose a significant risk of serious harm to others as a result of a mental disorder'. The proposals included 320 new high-security spaces in prisons and NHS institutions 'for those who are dangerous with severe personality disorder'; 75 community rehabilitation hostel places; and a programme of treatment research. The goal, the report indicated, is 'to identify those interventions which are most effective in addressing an individual's needs and which contribute to reductions in offending' (Home Office 2001a, 48).

Halliday extended the definition of dangerous offenders beyond just the mentally disordered. He proposed a 'special' sentence for dangerous offenders who presented 'high risks of re-offending and serious harm', were not dealt with under mental health legislation, and were not receiving life sentences. Halliday would limit the sentence's scope, however, to a small number of very serious violent and sexual crimes. He also stressed that the proposals were 'potentially very onerous and punitive' and that it would be important to ensure that they were 'not used inappropriately'. His proposal was that qualifying dangerous offenders would not be released on serving one-half of their sentences but could be kept in prison, at the discretion of the parole board, until their sentence expired and could then be subject to supervision for another five or ten years (Home Office 2001b: 33).

The White Paper revealed none of the narrowness of focus that characterized the pre-election document nor the caution and anxiety about overreach that characterized Halliday. Halliday's effort to balance liberty against danger disappeared. No effort was made in the White Paper to explain which offenders should be 'assessed as dangerous'. For those assessed as dangerous, however, the White Paper proposed that prison sentences be indeterminate and that prisoners be held until the Parole Board 'was completely satisfied' that the offender's 'risk had sufficiently diminished' (Home Office 2002a: 95). That is an impossible and therefore easily abused standard. The prison sentence could continue for the rest of the offender's life. Afterwards, if released from prison, the offender could remain on licence for the rest of his life. The White Paper's implicit premise is that there are no difficult trade-offs to be made between offenders' liberty and public safety.

The Criminal Justice Act pulled back a bit in some ways and went further in others. For particularly serious and some not-so-serious offences, the Act authorizes life sentences. For offenders convicted of offences bearing maximum sentences less than ten years, the offender may be held up to the maximum of the full sentence imposed, rather than be released at the mid-point, but importantly, the custodial term may not exceed that commensurate with the seriousness of the offence (and related offences). In other words, the White Paper notwithstanding, desert considerations are made relevant to the lengths of sentences for lesser 'dangerous' offenders. That's pulling back. The Act goes much further than Halliday, however, by identifying 153 offences, including some venial ones, as offences triggering the dangerous-offender provisions and their presumptions in favour of imprisonment and against release.

Extraordinary measures to deal with dangerous offenders, and related temporary sacrifices in procedural protections, at least arguably might be understandable if violence were becoming more common or more lethal, or if there were reason to believe that current laws and practices are inadequate. Awkwardly for the government, however, the opposites of those propositions are true. Violent crime rates declined during most of the 1990s and were far lower in 2003 than they were in 1993. The police and the courts already have broad powers for dealing with violent crime, and have been using these powers with increasing vigour. As Matravers and Hughes (2003) demonstrate in a recent essay on policies for dealing with serious sexual offences, crime rates are down, conviction rates are up, more offenders are being sent to prison, and sentences are longer. Data presented in Chapter 6 of this book show the same things.

With dangerous as with persistent offenders, the government's proposals are concerned more with symbols than with substance. No one questions that dangerous and persistent offenders present public policy challenges. No one questions the awfulness of the killings by Michael Stone, Roy Whiting or Ian Huntley. No one has, however, demonstrated that the policies that Labour has proposed are necessary, will make such horrible crimes any less likely to happen, or will accomplish anything important.

Theatre and symbols

The Labour government notoriously cares a great deal about focus groups and tabloid front pages, but more in relation to some subjects than to others. Private-sector partnerships, foundation hospitals, university top-up fees and Iraq are among the others. Crime and punishment is one of those subjects (political refugees is another) about which little is said or done without what looks like enormous concern for short-term public and media reactions. Chapter 3 considers reasons why that might be. This section provides illustrations (though in their separate ways, nearly every subject discussed in this book provides an illustration).

Horrible things sometimes happen. The killings of two little girls in Soham, the shootings of four Birmingham teenagers on New Year's Eve

2002, the 2000 murder of Sarah Payne, and the 1993 murder of Stephen Lawrence are examples. And sometimes particular crime problems become especially acute. The rapid rise in street robberies of mobile phones in 2000–02 is one example. Substantial recent increases in crimes involving firearms is another.

Governments do and should take account of horrible individual incidents and significant changes in important social problems. Expressions of sympathy for victims and survivors, avowals of intentions to think seriously about lessons that might be learned, appointment of task forces and commissions of enquiry – all of these things are commonly done and applauded. And if those processes generate well thought-out proposals for changes in laws or policies, so much the better.

The current Labour government, however, typically overreacts. Sometimes it rashly proposes poorly considered policy responses, many of which must quickly be abandoned. Since 2001, it has frequently convened 'summits', hyped-up media events meant to demonstrate its seriousness of purpose. Often the government appears mostly to be concerned to convey the impression that it is doing something.

Summits

'Summits' became in 2001–3 the symbol that the government takes a problem seriously. Table 2.1 shows crime summits convened between 1999 and early 2003, as reported in the broadsheets and tabloids. The pace quickened: one in 1999, two each in 2000 and 2001, between six and 20 in 2002, depending on how the Prime Minister's weekly street crime summits are counted, and two in the early weeks of 2003. Within weeks, for example, of the New Year's Eve Birmingham shootings, David Blunkett convened a summit on gun crime and shortly thereafter another one on gangsta rap. The attendees at the first were mostly police officers, prosecutors and probation personnel, along with a few 'community representatives'. The gangsta rap summit was attended mostly by politicians, Home Office officials and people from the music industry. Conspicuously absent from either were public health experts, researchers and policy analysts.

Opposition spokesmen and others typically characterize the summits, including the gun-crime summit, as 'knee-jerk' responses and media events. A few moments' thought about international affairs summits suggests that they are right. International summits are highly stylized but they are seldom last-minute improvisations.

Table 2.1 Crime summits, Labour Government, 1999–03

Topic	Date	Convener	Attendees	Source
Gangsta rap	15 January 2003	David Blunkett	music industry, Home Office	*Times*, 15 January 2003
Guns	10 January 2003	David Blunkett	CPS, police, customs, victims' families, DfES	*Observer*, 12 January 2003
Organized crime	November 2002	David Blunkett	Police, customs, Home Office	*Mail on Sunday*, 1 December 2002
Urban issues	November 2002	John Prescott	Local officials, police, Home Office	*Sunday Times*, 17 November 2002
Street crime	Various, March–September 2002	Tony Blair	Cabinet ministers, senior police, Home Office	*Times*, various dates
Crack cocaine	24 June 2002	David Blunkett	police, customs, treaters	*Times*, 24 June 2002
School violence	25 April 2002	Estelle Morris	Treasury, Education, Pensions Department, Home Office	*Guardian*, 23 April 2002
Violence	20 March 2002	Tony Blair	7 cabinet ministers, heads of law-enforcement agencies	*Guardian*, 21 March 2002
Police reform	29 January 2002	David Blunkett	43 chief constables and Bill Bratton	*Guardian*, 30 January 2002
Police reform	13 July 2001	David Blunkett	43 chief constables	*Daily Mail*, 21 March 2002
Street robbery	30 January 2001	Jack Straw	Police, mobile phone industry	*Guardian*, 16 January *2001*
Violent crime	3 July 2000	Tony Blair	Chief constables, ACPO	*Guardian*, 4 July 2001
Drugs	16 February 2000	Tony Blair	Jack Straw, Mo Mowlam, Drugs Czar, treaters, police	*Guardian*, 17 February 2001
International organized crime	November 1999	Tony Blair	Heads of MI5, MI6, and GCHQ; Home Office, police	

International summits are typically formal meetings of heads of state or senior ministers such as foreign or treasury secretaries. Usually they are preceded by months or years of staff work that includes negotiating terms of understandings, preparing and settling terms of agreements to be announced or signed, preparing agendas and working out protocol. Not much that's important happens at the meeting; it is a largely ceremonial occasion that gives each participant an opportunity to speak and to be photographed and recorded while doing so. The decisions 'reached' and publicly announced are negotiated and written up in advance. Summits sometimes are cancelled when it becomes apparent that acceptable agreement cannot be reached beforehand. The summit thus serves to demonstrate the high importance of the subject under consideration and to announce new agreements, understandings and aspirations. They are definitely media events, but they conclude and memorialize deliberations, not initiate them.

The January 2003 gun crime summit lacked any of the characteristics of an international summit. It was hastily convened in a setting in which it cannot have been possible to develop well-considered new proposals or policies. The knee-jerk quality of the event was demonstrated by Blunkett's contemporaneous announcement of a government proposal for a mandatory five-year sentence for any gun crime involving an illegal firearm. For a variety of reasons (over-breadth, judicial resistance, foreseeable unjustly long sentences in some cases), the proposal was not sound, as was demonstrated by Blunkett's concession within days that it would have to be modified to allow judges to ignore it when circumstances justified (that's how it was enacted).

Innumerable initiatives

An oft-quoted but perhaps apocryphal Chinese proverb: 'When much noise on stairs ... Nobody comes.' Throughout the Labour government's two terms in office, there has been much noise about criminal justice and related topics (especially antisocial behaviour). To some extent during Jack Straw's term as Home Secretary, but in much larger volumes since David Blunkett took over at Queen Anne's Gate, policy proposals and announcements of new initiatives tumble out. Many seem crafted primarily as a basis for issuing press releases and keeping the Home Office in the news. Table 2.2 summarizes some of the major initiatives announced by David Blunkett's Home Office between June 2001 and May 2003. The table would be several times larger if lesser initiatives were included.

Table 2.2 David Blunkett's major crime initiatives, June 2001–May 2003

Date	Source	Proposals
May 2003	*Daily Telegraph*, 17 May 2003	Householders to get greater protection from being sued by burglars injured committing their crimes.
	6 May 2003	Plans to develop biometric chips capable of storing details of the holder's fingerprints and iris patterns to be introduced in British passports in two years.
	7 May 2003	Three-tier sentencing system for murder: whole-life sentences for terrorist murders and for multiple murders showing premeditation, involving abduction, or which are sexual and sadistic; 30-year starting point for 'second category' murder, such as killing a policeman; 15-year tariff for other murders and for juveniles.
March 2003	*Daily Telegraph*, 13 March 2003	Publication of anti social behaviour White Paper, *Respect and Responsibility: Taking a Stand Against Anti-Social Behaviour*; proposals to extend the range of people with the power to issue fixed penalty notices of between £40 and £100 fines for adults to cover 16- and 17-year-olds and, possibly, younger children.
		Make it easier to evict antisocial tenants and prosecute fly-tippers; penalties for children who vandalise property and use airguns recklessly or fireworks dangerously.
February 2003	*Daily Telegraph*, 25 February 2003	Launch of the Assets Recovery Agency set up to seize the wealth of previously untouchable 'Mr Bigs'.
January 2003	*Daily Telegraph*, 30 January 2003	Range of legislative changes proposed in Sexual Offences Bill.

Table 2.2 continues opposite

Table 2.2 continued

Date	Source	Proposals
	Guardian, 6 January 2003	Change in Criminal Justice Bill to include five-year minimum prison sentence proposed for carrying illegal guns.
November 2002	*Daily Telegraph*, 26 November 2002	New sentencing framework announced.
	24 November 2002	Crackdown on 'sex tourists' including to seize the travel documents of the country's most serious offenders.
	20 November 2002	Publication of White Paper on sex offenders and sex offences, *Protecting the Public*; proposals to replace existing 'archaic, incoherent and discriminatory' legislation with at least 25 new offences.
	14 November 2002	Criminal Justice Bill announced: scrapping double-jeopardy; limiting access to jury trials in fraud cases and where intimidation was a risk; publication of bill to enact the new European arrest warrant.
	10 November 2002	Anti-Social Behaviour Bill will introduce on-the-spot fines for minor offences and streamline the use of antisocial behaviour orders (ASBOs).
October 2002	*Daily Telegraph*, 24 October 2002	Youth Inclusion and Support Panels comprised of a range of experts including the police and social services – to be set up over the next six months in 10 areas with the highest rate of street crimes.
	Guardian, 5 October 2002	Plans to give magistrates and judges targeted powers to jail for three months defendants who fail to show up, and

Table 2.2 continues overleaf

Table 2.2 continued

Date	Source	Proposals
		empower them to increase the severity of a non-custodial sentence as a punishment for failing to attend.
	Daily Telegraph, 3 October 2002	Plan to give powers to police to visit the homes of defendants an hour before they are due to appear in court; plan to increase police numbers by 3,000 in two years.
September 2002	*Daily Telegraph*, 17 September 2002	Plan for cutting police red tape to free up more officers for patrols.
July 2002	*Daily Telegraph*, 18 July 2002	Publication of Halliday sentencing review White Paper, *Justice For All*; announcement to scrap double jeopardy rule; limited access to jury trials; new Custody Plus/Minus and Intermittent Custody sentences; increase in magistrates' sentencing powers from 6 to 12 months' imprisonment.
	9 July 2002	Reclassification of cannabis from a Class B controlled drug to a Class C substance; maximum penalty for dealing in a Class C drug is to be doubled to 10 years.
June 2002	*Daily Telegraph*, 26 June 2002	Mental Heath Bill published, including proposal for indefinite detention of individuals with dangerous severe personality disorders.
May 2002	*Daily Telegraph*, 8 May 2002	Plan to make fine defaulters work off unpaid penalties through community work; plan to extend the prosecution's right to appeal against court decisions to grant bail.
April 2002	*Daily Telegraph*, 18 April 2002	£180 million from Treasury to help fight street crime and tackle prison over-

Table 2.2. continues opposite

Table 2.2 continued

Date	Source	Proposals
		crowding; additional £100 million, some of which will be used to provide 2,300 prison and juvenile remand places; wider powers to magistrates to lock up 12- to 16-year-olds.
	14 April 2002	New 'parenting contracts' in which parents of unruly children to be given formal warnings that they face large fines or the loss of their council home.
	11 April 2002	New Youth Offender Panels to tackle young criminals; video ID parades in robbery hot-spot areas.
March 2002	*Daily Telegraph,* 11 April 2002	Crackdown on crime hot-spots; further extension of ASBOs; new guidelines for tackling drug dealers on housing estates; action on street crime through a Robbery Reduction Initiative; new advisory panel for victims; fixed penalty fines for minor public order offences considered; ID cards; early release of prisoners on curfew.
February 2002	*Daily Telegraph,* 11 April 2002	Security boost for 3,000 shops in deprived areas; measures to tackle crack cocaine traffickers; moves to reduce delays and improve quality of prosecutions; credit card fraud initiative; tagging of young criminals on bail; car security campaign.
January 2002	*Daily Telegraph,* 11 April 2002	Plans to regulate the motor salvage industry; initiative to reduce burglary in deprived areas; implementation of measures to help vulnerable or intimidated witnesses give evidence in court; Police Reform Bill published.

Table 2.2. continues overleaf

Table 2.2 continued

Date	Source	Proposals
December 2001	*Daily Telegraph*, 11 April 2002	Radical reforms of the police; drugs and crime to be targeted by new community partnerships; national 'Rethinking Crime and Punishment' initiative.
November 2001	*Daily Telegraph*, 11 April 2002	Court orders to help offenders confront their drug problem.
October 2001	*Daily Telegraph*, 11 April 2002	£15 million regional security scheme to beat retail crime; extending the use of antisocial behaviour orders (ASBOs); top firms sign up to hi-tech drive to cut crime; new powers to search and seize criminal cash.
September 2001	*Daily Telegraph*, 11 April 2002	Computer-based training package to help protect homes; online campaign to cut car crime; strategy to stem the rising number of offences committed by women; new powers for the police to tackle crime.
August 2001	*Daily Telegraph*, 11 April 2002	Local child curfew extended to 15-year-olds; guidance to police for arresting kerb crawlers, hit and run drivers and pornography importers; £79 million CCTV investment for 250 new schemes; powers to tackle public drinking and prostitution.
July 2001	*Daily Telegraph*, 11 April 2002	Advice to mobile phone users; a £45 million programme to tackle persistent young offenders; smartcard technology to tackle credit card fraud; permanent powers to tackle football thugs; a task force to protect children on the Internet; commitment to make Britain 'the safest place in the world' for children to use the Internet.
June 2001	*Daily Telegraph*, 11 April 2002	£15 million to drive crime out of shopping centres.

A few of those initiatives are important. Some are worthy. Many are 'noise on the stairs'.

Serious policy processes are evidence-based, measured and cumulative. Serious media strategies are attention-grabbing and sensational. Looked at as a whole, the items in Table 2.2 appear much more to evidence a media than a criminal justice policy strategy.

Mobile phone robberies

The series of street violence summits called at No. 10 Downing Street by the Prime Minister also illustrate the improvisational nature of Labour government crime summits. They were precipitated by concern about increasing levels of street robberies, significantly driven by tabloid coverage of increased robberies of mobile phones. One Home Office report (Harrington and Mayhew 2001: 269) showed that robbery overall declined 3 per cent between 1999/2000 and 2000/2001, but mobile phone robberies increased by 96 per cent. A second Home Office report (Smith 2003: 540) showed that 43 per cent of all personal robberies in the police areas studied involved mobile phones.

Astonishingly, at a time when both official police data and the British Crime Survey's victimization data showed that overall crime rates were declining, the government, the judiciary, and the Metropolitan Police panicked. In January 2002, the Court of Appeal in an opinion by Lord Chief Justice Woolf held that a minimum 18-month prison sentence was appropriate for street robberies 'irrespective of the age of the offender' (important because a large proportion of offenders were children). In February, the Metropolitan Police diverted hundreds of officers from other duties to focus on street crime in eight London boroughs. Also in February, Tony Blair established a street crime committee and assigned ten ministers to oversee street crime initiatives in ten areas. In March, Blair convened the first of a series of multi-agency street crime meetings in Downing Street and David Blunkett initiated his Street Crime Initiative in which 5,000 officers were diverted from other duties. In April, Blair announced that street robbery would be under control by September. In May, 67 special fast-track street crime courts were established and the Crown Prosecution Service diverted experienced lawyers to deal with mugging cases and hired 60 new lawyers and 80 support staff to focus on muggings in ten street crime hot-spots (details are drawn from articles in the *Daily Telegraph*, 31 January, 18 March and 9 May 2003).

Not surprisingly, street robberies declined by September. All of the attention devoted to the subject probably played some role, but what statisticians call 'regression to the mean' also no doubt happened. Crime rates declined in the 1990s, and upwards 'blips' are more likely to be short-term anomalies than basic changes in direction. When they are anomalies, rates can be expected to revert to the underlying trends rather than remain high. The anomalous but short-lived phone robbery crisis was partly technological. Many phones carried programmed minutes and calls were not easily traceable, and for a time phones became a hot commodity. As soon as technological changes made phones less attractive commodities, however, phone robberies were bound to decline. And so they did – and so they would have done without all the theatrics.

Knee-jerk proposals

By the middle of 2002, the media and opposition spokesmen were regularly referring to Labour's summit announcements and crime-control pronouncements as knee-jerk, and more often than not nothing came afterwards. If, for a few months, the phrase 'knee-jerk' was considered a political term of art, it referred to hasty, and hastily repudiated, proposals from the Prime Minister, the Deputy Prime Minister, and the Home Secretary. Five such proposals, set out in Table 2.3, attracted particular attention. I briefly summarize their short half-lives here, but more interesting than *what* was proposed is *why* it was proposed.

The most celebrated proposal was offered in Tübingen, Germany, on 30 June 2000. The Prime Minister, at the inaugural session of the Global Ethics Foundation established by the German theologian Hans Kung, in his formal remarks announced: 'A thug might think twice about kicking in your gate, throwing traffic cones around your street, or hurling abuse into the night sky if he thought he might get picked up by the police, taken to a cashpoint and asked to pay an on-the-spot fine of, for example, £100' (*Guardian*, 1 July 2000).

Why was this proposed in Germany, and to an audience of theologians? Why 'thugs', when most people acting out in public under the influence of alcohol are a cross-section of the population, including famously, three days after the Tübingen speech, the Prime Minister's teenaged son Euan? Why would tossing about traffic cones, surely a venial offence except under extreme circumstances, and shouting into the night, seldom an offence at all, trigger such responses? And what

Table 2.3 Knee-jerk crime policy proposals, Labour government, 2000–03

Proposer	Proposal	Proposed	Abandoned	Sources
Tony Blair	On-the-spot fines for louts	July 2000	July 2000	*Guardian*, 4 July 2000
Tony Blair	Benefit cuts for truants' parents	April 2002	July 2002	*Times*, 19 July 2002
Tony Blair	Drug treatment in 24 hours for street robbers	May 2002	May 2002	*Guardian*, 10 May 2002
John Prescott	On-the-spot fines for dropping chewing gum on streets	November 2002	November 2002	*Sunday Times*, 17 November 2002
David Blunkett	Minimum 5-year sentence for all gun crimes	January 2003	January 2003	*Sunday Times*, 5 January 2003

about questions of natural justice and procedural fairness and the presumption of innocence?

None of these questions was ever answered because the proposal was soon abandoned. A 4 July 2000 *Guardian* story, under the headline, 'Police Push Blair into Yob Fines Climbdown', began: 'Tony Blair yesterday made one of his most humiliating climbdowns when he was forced by a revolt of Britain's top police officers to abandon his plan for £100 instant fines to tackle drunken louts only 72 hours after its launch.'

The second most notorious of the knee-jerk proposals, proposed by the Prime Minister at a meeting of the Street Crime Action Group (one of the street crime summits) on 10 April 2002, called for, according to the *Sunday Telegraph* (5 May 2002), 'a highly controversial plan to withdraw child benefit payments from parents of persistent truants and offenders'. Here, too, a whole series of questions arises. Wouldn't that be a form of vicarious or collective punishment, which all human rights conventions and notions of natural justice forbid? Persistent truants typically come from the most deprived and socially disadvantaged families, and can it possibly be sensible social policy to make their families even more deprived?

As with on-the-spot fines for yobs, however, these questions never needed to be addressed. According again to the *Sunday Telegraph*, the proposal was soon abandoned because:

> almost the entire Cabinet refused to play along. Not only was the Prime Minister's policy attacked in private, but no minister appeared willing to give even lukewarm support in public ... It soon became apparent that most of the cabinet thought that Mr Blair's idea was ill-judged at best, or even half-baked.

The other best-known proposals and ensuing climbdowns can briefly be described. In May 2002, the Prime Minister proposed that all drug-dependent street robbers be placed in drug treatment within 24 hours. This is not an inherently bad idea in terms of policy or principle; it's just unworkable. Since waiting lists for admission to drug treatment programmes then required a five-month wait, the policy would have created perverse incentives for addicts to commit robberies in order to get into treatment and would have caused those on the list who were not committing crimes to wait even longer.

The final two are Deputy Prime Minister John Prescott's November 2002 proposal that dustmen be authorized to impose on-the-spot fines on people who drop chewing gum on the street, and Home Secretary David Blunkett's January 2003 proposal that anyone convicted of any crime involving an illegal gun receive a mandatory minimum five-year prison sentence. The first was quickly dropped as preposterous and the second was quickly modified because judges made it clear they would oppose it unreservedly and others pointed out that it would inevitably result in imposition of notorious and indefensible sentences on ordinary people who had done innocuous things.

* * * *

If the Labour government's criminal justice policies were evaluated with evidence-based calipers, many would receive failing marks. On low-visibility, technocratic issues like alteration of charging practices, or uncontroversial offend-no-one subjects like enriching victims' services, evidence and humane values appear to matter. For issues that are at all controversial, that might attract tabloid wrath or Tory resistance, however, symbols and rhetoric count for much more than substance. The next chapter considers why that is so, and why, save for those of the United States, English punishment policies are now the harshest in Western Europe, North America, and the Antipodes.

Chapter 3

English exceptionalism

Until the early 1990s criminal justice policy in England was not highly politicized. Conservatives in the 1970s began to raise crime as a campaign issue, but criminal justice policy was little affected. Between 1987 and 1992, crime rates grew by 50 per cent and the prison population fell from 50,000 to 40,000 (Downes and Morgan 2002).

Law and order 'were relatively insulated from the realm of party politics for so long', Downes and Morgan (2002: 287) write, because of 'the strength of the belief that crime, like the weather, is beyond political influence; and that the operation of the law and criminal justice should be above it'. Where has that belief gone, and why?

The short answer is that Tony Blair and the Labour Party have modelled their criminal justice politics and policies on those of Bill Clinton and his New Democratic Coalition. Democratic presidential candidate Michael Dukakis's loss in 1988 is generally believed to have happened in significant part because he was seen as soft on crime. Clinton in 1992, reports the *Washington Post* (Slevin 2000), was 'determined not to take second place in anyone's toughness on crime poll'. He talked tough and, in a melodramatic gesture, flew home to Arkansas after a presidential debate to preside over the execution of brain-damaged Ricky Ray Rector, who had shot himself in the head in remorse immediately after shooting a police officer in a bungled robbery. Rector was so mentally impaired that, at his last supper, the night before he was to be executed at dawn, he set aside his dessert so he could have it with lunch the next day. Rector died so that Clinton could prove his toughness. 'You can't law-and-order Clinton,' said Jay

Jacobsen, a former Arkansas prosecutor. 'If you can kill Rector, you can kill anybody' (LaFranière 1992).

Throughout Clinton's presidency, he and his advisors stuck to the tough-on-crime position. In 1994, for example, he supported and signed into law an omnibus federal crime bill that made 60 additional federal crimes punishable by death, created a federal 'three-strikes-and-you're-out' law, and authorized $8 billion in prison-construction dollars to states that would toughen their sentencing laws.

It worked. Crime was not a major issue in the 1996 and 2000 presidential races: 'Many Democrats have started to sound more like Republicans by supporting stricter punishment, more policing, and, often, the death penalty' (Slevin 2000). Ed Rogers, the deputy campaign manager in 1988 for George Bush the elder, in 2000 admitted that the Democrats 'finally got the message, politically speaking, the tougher the better on crime. There hasn't been much room between their rhetoric and ours' (Slevin 2000).

The Labour Party as early as the 1992 elections began to emulate the Clinton approach. According to Lord Windlesham, reporting on parliamentary deliberations on what became the Criminal Justice Act 1993, 'Even when Labour put forward amendments which would have tempered the severity of proposals in the Bill, they often seemed anxious to couch their arguments in "tougher than thou" style' (Windlesham 1996: 66). In the 1997 general election, 'Labour claimed now to be the party of "law and order"' (Downes and Morgan 2002: 293). And, also parallelling the American experience, 'In neither the 1997 nor the 2001 elections were law and order issues prominent' (Downes and Morgan 2002: 291).

The Labour approach to crime that Downes and Morgan describe remains in effect. Proposals for ever-tougher policies, new 'initiatives' every week or two, 'summits' convened on the least pretext – all these continued into 2003. This can be seen in Tables 2.1, 2.2 and 2.3, where I show media-attention-catching knee-jerk policy proposals that were launched to divert attention from awkward news stories and then quickly dropped, the increasing frequency of crime summits in 2001 and 2002, and two years' worth of new initiatives announced by Home Secretary David Blunkett. But also in Chapter 2, I refer to reports that even the Prime Minister considers some of the policies proposed and adopted to be 'horrible', even if they are believed to be politically necessary.

That account of Labour's anti-crime strategy is alright as far as it goes, but it doesn't explain why Labour thought it necessary or why it worked. American crime-control policies, after all, are by a wide margin the harshest in any Western country, and England's traditionally have been comparable with those of other large European countries (Germany, France, Italy) and of English-speaking countries other than the US (Canada, Australia). Until the early 1990s, English crime policies and imprisonment rates were in the Western mainstream. In most Western countries, crime is not a high-salience political issue and leading parties are not stalemated at the harshest credible policy positions. So what is it about England that makes it the only major Western country to emulate American anti-crime politics and policies?

A variety of explanations have been offered. The two commonest are, first, a particularly vulgar form of political cynicism – Clintonite demagoguery worked and Blair decided to do the same thing – and, second, punitive public attitudes: the public wanted toughness and Labour gave it to them. These may be tolerable descriptions but they can't be adequate explanations. Politicians are everywhere pusillanimous, but there is no reason to suppose English politicians are more cynical and self-interested than those in other European countries. And public opinion in all Western countries has become less tolerant of crime and more punitive toward criminals over the past decade (e.g., Roberts *et al.* 2003). So there is nothing special about English politicians or public attitudes that explains why crime politics and policies are so different from those in, say, Canada or Germany or Italy. The explanation must lie elsewhere.

A number of possible explanations for what might be called 'English exceptionalism' can be dismissed out of hand. Rises in crime rates are one example. Crime rates rose in every Western country from the 1960s through the early or mid-1990s – England, Holland, Switzerland, Sweden, the United States, Canada, Australia, to name countries almost at random – and then fell (van Kesteren *et al.* 2000; Farrington *et al.* 2004). The pattern was the same everywhere – in big countries, small countries, Western European countries, Eastern European countries, countries in other regions. Crime patterns in England that are the same as those everywhere can't explain why English politics and policies have developed differently from those elsewhere.

Nor can the politics of race and ethnicity. Plausible arguments can be made in the United States that considerations of race shaped crime policies that the Labour government is racing to emulate, but making that case is difficult in England. No one seriously denies that Republicans in the US long pursued a 'Southern strategy' that sought to use racial appeals to separate white southerners and working-class voters more generally from their traditional Democratic loyalties

(Phillips 1970; Edsall and Edsall 1991). Issues like crime, welfare and affirmative action (in England, 'positive discrimination') – all at face-value generic policy subjects – were used to appeal to racial stereotypes. The paradigm cases were the Reagan adminstration's characterization of a black Chicago woman, Linda Taylor, as a high-living 'welfare queen' who personified the problems of welfare, and the first Bush administration's use of black murderer and rapist Willie Horton to personify the Democrats' weakness on crime (Anderson 1995; Tonry 1995, chap. 1). The texts of these campaigns, it might be said, were about welfare and crime but the subtexts were about race. Put differently, welfare fraud and violent crime were given black faces.

There are a number of reasons why the race analysis doesn't work for England. Most importantly, race relations have not been the galvanizing issue in English politics for a half-century as they have been in the United States. Mainstream politicians in both major American parties regularly and openly made racist appeals to white voters for most of the twentieth century, some as recently as the 1980s. In England, open appeals to racial bias and animus have come only from the political fringes. Lord Woolf, not slow to accuse politicians of demagoguery in relation to sentencing (Woolf 1999),[1] has observed, 'On the whole the politicians are very good about race; they don't approve of what is called playing the race card' (Dodd 2000).

Almost as importantly, Afro-Caribbeans constitute less than 3 per cent of the English population. Even though in relative terms they are more likely than whites or Asians to be arrested for violent and drug crimes, and as a group have higher imprisonment rates, in absolute terms their contributions to English crime rates and prison populations are small. In the United States, where nearly half of those arrested for violent crimes and nearly half of those in prison are black, politicians pandered to white voters' stereotypes about and fears of black criminals (Tonry 1995: chaps. 2 and 3). Nothing comparable happened in England; the face of the stereotypical criminal is white and working class.

Finally, by international standards, the involvement in crime of members of ethnic and racial minority groups in England is nothing special. In every country, members of some disadvantaged minority groups are over-represented among criminals and prisoners. The identities of the groups vary between countries. In some places, such as France, Belgium and the Netherlands, they are North Africans. In others, such as Canada, Australia and New Zealand, they are descendants of aboriginal populations. Elsewhere, as in Germany and much of Scandinavia, they are people from West Asian countries like

Turkey, Iraq and Afghanistan, the Balkans, and the former Eastern Europe (Tonry 1997). Ethnic and racial tensions exist everywhere, and fringe politicians make xenophobic appeals. These things happen in England too, but not on a scale or with a degree of emotion to make racial politics a plausible explanation for Labour's crime policies.

So what is left if crime rates, public opinion, race relations and unusually pusillanimous politicians are ruled out? The rest of this chapter offers answers. First, English culture is more risk-averse than other Western cultures. People feel aggrieved and threatened by crime and are especially susceptible to law-and-order appeals. This may be a perverse and unintended side-effect of two decades' governmental focus on crime-prevention initiatives. Second, English culture accords little respect to offenders as human beings entitled to equal respect and concern, and human rights values therefore play less of a restraining influence than elsewhere on the treatment of offenders and prisoners. Third, English cultural values are more punitive toward offenders than are those of many other Western countries.

These, however, are only background conditions. They neither explain nor justify Labour's crime-control policies. They may explain why English society acquiesces in current policy but they cannot provide ethical justification for it.

Risk aversion

Newcomers to England, and tourists, are typically surprised by how much attention is paid to crime and crime prevention. CCTV is everywhere: on city streets, in shops, in staircases, in the forecourts of petrol stations, in parks, in parking garages, even around many private homes. So too are speed-trap cameras ubiquitous. Evening drives through the countryside are jarringly disrupted by the glare and then the presence of harsh orange lights at rural intersections. Nearly every car park has signs warning, 'Thieves operate here. Lock your car' and most are as brightly lighted at night as football stadiums. Police control the separate routes specified for opposing teams' fans into and out of football stadiums in order to prevent fights and brawls. Neighbourhood Watch signs festoon trees everywhere, including in tiny Cotswolds and Shropshire and Cumbrian villages from which crime is nearly absent.

Walking in Cambridge the day I wrote these words, I was taken aback to see that police had roped a sign to a tree on the genteel lawn of

Robinson College saying, 'Warning: Thieves active here.' A few years ago when I lived in Oxford, to amuse myself as I walked home through a prosperous part of north Oxford, I kept track of the percentages of parked cars with detachable metal steering-wheel locks. I tried to devise theories to explain why the percentages seemed to vary regularly with the day of the week. Seldom was the percentage below 50.

In the early 1990s, I used to compare England favourably with the United States for its investment in situational and community crime prevention rather than in expansion of the criminal justice system (e.g., Tonry and Farrington 1995). I thought that England was civilized, and hard-headed, and humane. Now I think England's massive and continuing investment in crime prevention a mistake.

People who are constantly reminded that they should be fearful and protect themselves from criminals *become* fearful; and that may make them more likely to be more mistrustful and more receptive to populist anti-crime appeals. And, having through assiduous crime-prevention programmes created a more fearful populace, England is now busily expanding its criminal justice system to address those fears. The worst of both worlds.

There is some empirical evidence, mostly from successive International Crime Victims Surveys, that suggests that people living in the United Kingdom generally and England and Wales in particular worry more about crime than people in other Western countries, and think more about crime prevention. The International Crime Victims Survey, hereafter referred to as the ICVS, is a series of representative surveys of the populations of participating countries. Respondents are asked about victimization by crime, fear of crime, crime-prevention efforts, and whether and why they do and don't report crimes to the police, among other things.

English and UK victimization rates for burglary and car theft tend to be among the highest but, overall, crime rates for England, Scotland and Northern Ireland fall towards the middle among the dozen or so countries that regularly participate. Even so, fear of crime is highest among British citizens. In the first, 1989, survey, for example, fear of street crime in England was second highest among 14 participating countries, and England and Scotland were first and second among 14 countries in the percentage of single-family homes protected by burglar alarms (van Dijk *et al*. 1990: figs. 38 and 43).

The pattern shown in 1989 continued thereafter, with comparative UK fear of crime and investment in private crime-prevention initiatives becoming steadily more pronounced. In 1992, the percentage of respondents in England feeling unsafe after dark was second highest among six Western European countries, and in 1996 the percentages in England and Scotland feeling unsafe were first and second among 11 countries (nine in Europe plus the US and Canada). In both 1992 and 1996, higher percentages of English respondents had burglar alarms on their homes than anywhere else, and in both years nearly three-quarters of English and Scottish homes had one or more of burglar alarms, special locks or window or door grilles (much higher than elsewhere) (van Dijk and Mayhew 1992: fig. 25; Mayhew and van Dijk 1997: figs. 13 and 14, tables 17 and 18).

The same patterns obtained in the most recent ICVS. Again in 2000, a higher percentage of English respondents said they felt unsafe alone at night out of doors in their area than did respondents from eight other Western European countries. And also in 2000, more English respondents' homes had burglar alarms than in any of the other 15 countries, and by a wide margin, with Scotland tied for second (van Kesteren *et al.* 2000: tables 17 and 18 and fig. 14).

The British Crime Survey gives striking evidence of the perverse effects of overemphasis on crime and crime prevention concerning antisocial behaviour, a particular preoccupation of the Labour government. Table 3.1 shows percentages of British Crime Survey respondents who thought particular types of disorder were very or fairly big problems, at two-year intervals between 1992 and 1998 and annually since 2000. For most of the behaviours, the percentages fell or were flat until 1998, when the government began trumpeting its campaign against antisocial behaviour and enacted the Crime and Disorder Act 1998, and have risen markedly and steadily ever since (Simmons and Dodd 2003: table 8.12).

By making antisocial behaviour into a major social policy problem, and giving it sustained high-visibility attention, Labour has made a small problem larger, thereby making people more aware of it and less satisfied with their lives and their government.

Labour's general emphasis on the failings of the justice system have likewise, counterfactually, increased public fear of crime. After the years of declining crime rates that began in the mid-1990s, public belief that the national crime rate was a little or a lot worse declined to the lowest level in a decade in 2001. That year also contained the first of the major Labour documents and white papers on crime. Curiously, though crime rates have continued to fall, increasing percentages of people believe it is rising (from 25 per cent believing there is a lot more crime in 2001 to 38 per cent in 2003; from 31 per cent believing there is a little more in 2001 to 35 per cent in 2003) (Simmons and Dodd 2003: table 8.01).

Table 3.1 Trends in disorder perceived to be a 'very' or 'fairly' big problem, 1992 to 2002/03

Percentages	British Crime Survey							
	1992	1994	1996	1998	2000	2001	2001/02	2002/03
Noisy neighbours or loud parties	8	8	8	8	9	9	10	10
Teenagers hanging around on the streets	20	26	24	27	32	31	32	33
Rubbish or litter lying around	30	26	26	28	30	32	32	33
Vandalism, graffiti and other deliberate damage to property	26	29	24	26	32	34	34	35
People being attacked/harassed because of their race/colour	3	5	5	5	8	9	9	8
People using or dealing drugs	14	22	21	25	33	30	31	32

Source: BCS 1992 to 2002/03.

The ICVS and British Crime Survey evidence that people in England and Scotland are becoming more fearful, and think crime problems are getting worse, dovetails nicely with analyses offered by sociologist David Garland (2001). He suggests that what might be called 'post-modernist angst' lies behind contemporary English and American crime policies, and public acceptance of them. He identifies four contributing factors.

First, crime is more widely distributed than in the past, and avoidance of crime has become a routine feature of everyday life:

> [B]y the 1970s society's vulnerability to high rates of crime came to be viewed for what it was – a normal social fact ... Whatever successes police and politicians may claim, crime avoidance remains a prominent organizing principle of everyday life.
>
> (2001: 194)

Victimization is no longer primarily localized in low-income, disadvantaged and minority neighborhoods. It is more evenly distributed and threatens affluent and middle-class people. Better-off people find themselves spending money and time trying to protect themselves and their property.

Second, although governments realize that they cannot do much about crime, they must pretend that they can. Crime's ubiquity exposed the 'myth that the sovereign state is capable of delivering "law and order" and controlling crime' (2001, 109). This created a predicament for policy-makers. They can accept the limits of their power, or they can pretend not to know them and 'retreat into an *expressive* mode ... that is concerned not so much with controlling crime as with expressing the anger and outrage that crime provokes' (2001: 110; emphasis in original).

Third, the new social fact of crime, particularly as it impinges on the middle class, importantly exacerbates the 'sense of ontological insecurity' of our time (2001: 155):

> [T]his new element of precariousness and insecurity is built into the fabric of everyday life ... Little surprise too that people increasingly demand to know about the risks to which they are exposed by the criminal justice system and are increasingly impatient when the system fails to control 'dangerous' individuals.
>
> (2001: 155)

Fourth is Garland's *'criminology of the other*, of the threatening outcast, the fearsome stranger, the excluded and the embittered [that] ... functions to demonize the criminal, to act out popular fears, and to promote support for state punishment' (2001: 137; emphasis in original). The outcasts in the social and political climates of the 1980s and 1990s inevitably were the welfare poor, urban blacks and marginalized working-class boys. These groups became scapegoats, and doing something to them and about them could be portrayed as doing something about crime.

So, putting all this together, why are harsh expressive policies adopted? Garland writes:

> Because the groups most affected lack political power and are widely regarded as dangerous and undeserving; because the groups least affected could be reassured that something is being done and lawlessness is not tolerated; and because few politicians are willing to oppose a policy when there is so little political advantage to be gained by doing so.
>
> (2001: 132)

The fundamental failing in Garland's account is that all of the developments he describes characterize every prosperous Western country, but the political and policy responses he describes have occurred primarily in England and America. Why have they affected those countries as they have, but not Canada, Germany, France and Sweden (a foursome picked almost at random)?

The American and English answers are different. This book is about English criminal justice policies, so I won't say much about the US. I address that subject in another book (Tonry 2004). There the answers relate to the volatility of American culture and politics, long-term cycles of tolerance and intolerance, racial dimensions of American politics, and the partisan elections of judges and prosecutors at city and county levels. The English answer has partly to do with fears generated by overemphasis on crime and crime prevention by government and the media, but also on a cultural taste (shared with the US) for the debasement of offenders, and a second cultural taste for punishment.

Debasement

English (and American) people seem better able to endure the suffering of others, especially of criminals, than are citizens of most Western countries. England's place at the top of the European rankings for incarceration rates is one bit of evidence. Another is English tolerance of prison conditions – slopping out (until recently), double- and triple-celling, overcrowding, high suicide rates, staff brutality – that most of Europe, and all of Europe from the Benelux countries north, would regard as *prima facie* violations of human rights.

Historian James Whitman offers an historical explanation for this cultural taste for prisoners' suffering. Whitman set out to understand why 'over the last quarter century, America has shown a systematic drive toward increased harshness by most measures, while [France and Germany] have not' (Whitman 2003: 38). One explanation is that 'American-style politics has failed to exert an American-style influence in German or French criminal justice,' and, as a result, 'bureaucrats have succeeded in keeping control of the punishment process, without becoming subject to decisive pressure from a stirred-up public' (2003: 15). England is not America, but much of Whitman's analysis contrasts English and American experience with those of France and Germany and helps explain recent English developments. And, unlike France and Germany, England has emulated American anti-crime policies and politics.

France and Germany have experienced rising crime rates, economic destabilization, more punitive public attitudes, ethnic tensions, and postmodernist angst no less than have England and the United States, and yet 'as of the year 2000, mildness is still, at heart, the watchword of punishment practices in each country' (p. 70). Whitman's *description* of contemporary differences between continental Europe and America is not an *explanation*. For that he goes back two centuries and identifies two differences between Europe and America that reverberate in our time. The first is the American distrust of government and government officials that developed in the 50-year build-up to the American Revolution and has characterized Americans ever since. This he contrasts to the strong European states of the eighteenth century and the continuation of support for strong states today. Germany and France have state apparatuses that, compared with American government, are relatively powerful and relatively autonomous. I return to this below, because England also has (and has traditionally had) a powerful central government, and might therefore be expected to resemble continental countries rather than the United States. As the quotation from Downes and Morgan (2002) that begins this chapter demonstrates, until little more than a decade ago, English criminal justice policy did more resemble Europe's than America's.

The second difference relates to the ways European and Anglo-

American societies ameliorated the consequences of seventeenth- and eighteenth-century status differentiation. Social hierarchy and status differences were, of course, marked in Europe, Britain and the American colonies, and extended to the ways people accused and convicted of crimes were dealt with. Status mattered, and can be illustrated by the forms of execution and imprisonment. Hangings are unattractive: the victim slowly asphyxiates, the bowels let loose, and the body is wracked with spasms. Beheadings are nearly instantaneous and the headless body, if supported, stays in place while the head tumbles out of sight into a basket. In Britain and Europe, low-status people were hanged; high-status people were beheaded. And so with prisons: low-status people were kept in crowded, squalid places while high-status people were allowed comfortable apartments in which to entertain visitors and be cared for by personal servants.

Whitman describes starkly different ways that Europe and Anglo-America responded to the status hierarchy in punishment. Europe levelled up, aspiring to treat all offenders with respect and civility, at least in principle as high-status prisoners formerly had been. England and America levelled down, treating all prisoners as persons not deserving respect and solicitude. In this framework, Whitman argues that much American [and English] punishment is degrading, as low-status punishment has always been degrading, while French and German punishment is premised on treating prisoners with respect and sympathy. Similarly, Whitman argues, American [and modern English] levelling-down egalitarianism leads to beliefs in the desirability of uniform and mandatory punishments, while the European response to historic anti-egalitarianism leads to beliefs in individualization and compassion.

The national differences Whitman describes in treatment of prisoners are easy to see. French and German prisoners wear everyday street clothes. English and American prisoners often wear uniforms. Prison guards in Germany are civil servants who complete a two-year course before beginning work. English and American officers are hired off the street. English and American inmates are subject to continuous surveillance. Cell doors nearly always contain glass vision panels or barred openings. German courts forbid the use of such doors, because they deny to prisoners the basic human right of privacy. German and French prisoners have all the rights of citizenship except those inherently incompatible with confinement. They are, for example, entitled to vote and polling stations are set up inside the prison. English and American prisoners are denied the right to vote. In other words, English and American prisoners are denied basic rights of citizenship and continental prisoners are treated as citizens behind bars.

Whitman's historical arguments are novel and creative. His depiction of differences between modern American and German approaches to criminal justice, however, is not new.

German sociologist Joachim Savelsberg (1994), now at the University of Minnesota, has described similar differences. He attributes the rationalistic and restrained German approach to a widely held view among elites of all mainstream political parties that issues of justice should be addressed on the basis of informed opinion and professional experience, and not on the basis of opinion polls or election returns. He contrasts this with American distrust of experts and willingness to subject almost every issue to the influence of raw public opinion, however well or poorly informed.

I've also discussed those differences (Tonry 1999; 2004: chaps 1, 8) and, accepting Savelsberg's characterization as accurate, attribute them in significant part in addition to American constitutional arrangements. Most judges and prosecutors are elected in partisan elections at local levels and many aspire to higher political office. The politicization of criminal justice policy that has occurred, largely as a product of the long-term Republican 'Southern strategy', has meant that no issue is off-limits to emotional and demagogic appeals. Nearly all prosecutors and distressingly many judges feel obliged to focus their campaigns on their toughness. As the Clinton story shows, tough-on-crime proved a winning issue. In most of Europe, including Germany and France, judges and prosecutors are career civil servants, far removed and insulated from partisan political campaigns, and possessed of professional values that decry political influence on issues of justice in individual cases.

Whitman's two theories, about strong and weak states, and punishment systems that level up or level down, fit nicely with contemporary differences in punishment systems. France and Germany grant autonomous officials substantial authority to individualize mild punishments. America, and to a lesser extent, England, attempt through legislation to limit the discretion of officials to deviate from comparatively uniform systems of harsh punishments.

What is odd, though, is that English constitutional arrangements, methods of selecting judges and prosecutors, and professional legal culture much more resemble those of Europe than of the United States, and yet its criminal justice policies have fallen prey to what might be called the 'American disease'. In effect, for England, Whitman's strong central- state hypothesis offsets his levelling-down hypothesis. English policy-makers could, had they wished to do so, have kept criminal justice policy-making in the hands of professionals, and for many years did just that. Labour in the early 1990s chose to abandon the insulated English governmental conventions and traditions in favour of rawer anti-crime politics patterned on the recent political history of the United States. That prisoners are widely seen in England as people whose interests do not warrant respect and concern may have made this easier to accomplish than it would be in continental Europe.

Punitiveness

Here my argument becomes more speculative. I believe a deeper strain of moralistic self-righteousness and punitiveness towards deviance and deviants characterizes British and American culture, especially their judiciaries, than is the case in other countries.

The International Crime Victims Survey offers some evidence that British culture is closer to American than to most of Europe in punitiveness of attitudes towards offenders. When asked in 1989 about the appropriate sentence for a recidivist burglar, the highest percentages of respondents favouring imprisonment were Americans (52.7), Northern Irish (45.4), Scots (39), and English (38.2). The average for all European countries was 22 per cent and for five (Germany, Switzerland, France, Norway and Finland), the percentage was 15 or lower (van Dijk *et al*. 1990: table 9).

In 1996, when the question was asked again in 10 countries, the American (56%), English (49%), Northern Irish (49%), and Scottish (48%) respondents most favoured imprisonment, and other Europeans least favoured it – Switzerland (9%), Austria (10%), France (11%), Finland (18%) (Mayhew and van Dijk 1997: table 10).

The same pattern continued in 2000. Among 16 countries, US respondents were likeliest to favour a prison sentence (56%) but Northern Ireland (54%), Scotland (52%), and England (51%) were next. In most European countries, between 12 and 21 per cent favoured prison sentences. And among European countries, English respondents would have imposed the longest sentences (van Kesteren *et al*. 2000: table 19).

Although every Home Secretary from Michael Howard to the present has declared his belief that 'prison works', the English judiciary appears to be at the heart of the problem. Martin Narey, the director of the Correctional Service of England and Wales, referred in a May 2002 speech before the Prison Reform Trust to the courts' 'continuing love affair with custody'. He warned, 'We simply cannot keep building ahead of this thirst for custody' (Travis 2002).

This is nothing new. Ian Dunbar and Andrew Langdon describe it as a pervasive problem: 'The courts have usually overfilled whatever prison capacity has been available' (1998: 59).

The judicial taste for punishment is beyond the reach even of the Lord Chief Justice. As Table 3.2 shows, at least nine times between December 2000 and December 2002, Lord Woolf publicly called upon English judges to send fewer people to prison and to impose shorter terms. Some of these calls were made in major public speeches. At other times they appeared in decisions of the Court of Appeal.

The result? None whatever. English judges continued decade-long patterns of increasing the percentages of convicted offenders sentenced to custody and lengthening the terms to be served. David Blunkett (2004: 9) has noted that 'the key explanation for the growth in the use of prison has been increased severity in sentencing'.

A Prison Reform Trust analysis confirmed this. Between 1991 and 2001, the custody rate in magistrates courts tripled, from five to sixteen per cent of sentences. In Crown Courts, the custody rate increased by half, from 46 to 64 per cent of cases, and sentences, especially for serious crimes, became much harsher (Hough, Jacobson and Millie 2003: 21). The Carter Report reports similar data, including that the likelihood of a first-time burglar receiving a prison sentence doubled between 1995 and 2000 (Carter 2003).

The taste for punishment is, however, not limited to the judiciary. English (and American) readers can, I suspect, confirm this for themselves by looking at Figure 3.1, and asking whether they approve the French policy choices it shows. The figure shows imprisonment rates per 100,000 citizens for England and France since 1968. The line showing English rates undulates before beginning a continuous upward trajectory in the mid-1990s. The French line zig-zags. This is because French governments, whether Socialist or Gaullist, from time to time decide to release large numbers of prisoners.

France periodically reduces its prison population substantially by means of broad-based commutations and amnesties. These typically occur on the inauguration of a new president or to celebrate a major occasion such as the 200th anniversary of the storming of the Bastille, but sometimes the nominal cause for celebration is less momentous. As Figure 3.1 shows, several of the broad-based pardons coincide with steep reductions in the imprisonment rate.

The periodic releases of large numbers of French prisoners have ameliorated what would otherwise be inexorable increases in the

Table 3.2 Lord Woolf's 'talking down the prison population', 2000–2002

Date	Where	Source	Exhortation
19 December 2002	Judgement, Court of Appeal	*Times*, 20 December 2002	Burglars facing a sentence of up to 18 months should not go to prison but be given a non-custodial supervised sentence. When a prison sentence was imposed, Lord Woolf said it should be 'no longer than necessary.'
29 October 2002	The 2002 Rose Lecture, Manchester	*Times*, 30 October 2002	'The problem of overcrowding in prisons is a cancer eating at the ability of the Prison Service to deliver'.
			'It is now accepted on all sides that prisons can do nothing for prisoners who are sentenced to less than 12 months.'
8 July 2002	Annual Review of the Court of Appeal	*Times*, 9 July 2002	'Ten years ago it [prison population] was 40,000. I would be very glad to see it fall back to 40,000'.
			'We're spending more and more money building more and more prisons to keep them at more and more expense without tackling the root of the problem. Probation and Prison Services can reduce the prison population.'
20 June 2002	Speech to conference	*Guardian*, 21 June 2002	'It is my firm belief we should send to prison fewer offenders. This does not mean serious offenders should not be imprisoned – they should be and, in some cases, the sentences need to be severe'.
		Times	Judges should recognize that 'they have no option but to confine the use of prison sentences to those offenders for

			whom there is no alternative and when they pass sentence, they [should] ensure they are no longer than necessary.'
5 March 2002	Judgement, Court of Appeal	*Guardian*, 6 March 2002	'The stage has been reached when it would be highly undesirable if the prison population were to continue to rise.'
			'We trust all courts will heed the message which the appeal court is giving today. That message is imprisonment only when necessary and for no longer than necessary.'
24 January 2002	Judgement, Court of Appeal	*Times*, 25 February 2002	Lord Woolf called for fewer women to be imprisoned when he overturned the sentence of a woman jailed for eight months for obtaining services by deception. He imposed a six-month community rehabilitation order.
25 October 2001	Speech to Youth Justice Board	*Guardian*, 25 October 2001	'It is a very simple message: Don't send people to prison unless it is really necessary.'
30 January 2001	Prison Reform Trust Lecture	*Times*, 1 February 2001	'If an analogy with a disease is appropriate, and I think it is, then I would describe overcrowding as the AIDS virus of the Prison Service. First, it debilitates the whole system. Secondly, we are still struggling to find a cure, notwithstanding the expenditure of vast sums of money.'
27 December 2000	Interview, BBC Radio	*Guardian*, 28 December 2000	'Overcrowding of prisons is a cancer which undermines the work of the prisons and the problem is we have people there because of the system who should not be there, who contribute to overcrowding.'

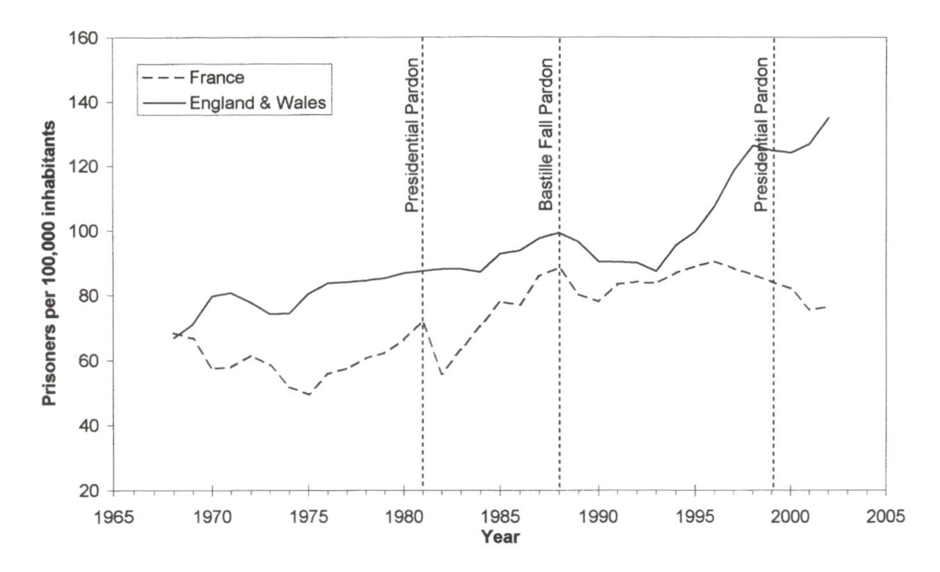

Figure 3.1 Incarceration rates in France and England and Wales, 1968–2002 (per 100,000 population).
Source: British National Statistical Office, Annual Abstract (various years), French Ministry of Justice, Series Pènitentiaires Temporelles (SEPT)

number of French prisoners. If, to adjust for year-to-year changes, the French imprisonment rate were calculated as a rolling five-year average, the resulting line would be close to flat, but because of the wholesale releases it moves rapidly up and down. If, however, the commutations and amnesties had not occurred, French imprisonment rates would have increased steadily and be as high as or higher than those in England.

Lord Woolf repeatedly, the Lord Chancellor and David Blunkett occasionally, and other Home Office ministers from time to time attempt to 'talk down' the prison population. Occasionally in recent years, as with the system of early release from prison into home detention backed by electronic tagging, programmmes have been established with the aim of diverting people from prison. The French approach is much faster, less costly, and foolproof. An English equivalent could quickly be devised. Release dates for all prisoners, for example, could be advanced by, say six months, or all sentences of whatever length could be reduced by a third.

What are the odds that the English government will soon announce a 10–30 per cent reduction in the prison population as the result of a broad-based programme of pardons or commutations? None.

Why? The government wouldn't dare, from fear of the tabloids' reactions and public disapproval, and because of likely judicial reaction. The tabloid and public reaction would likely be outrage that offenders were 'getting off easy'. Academics and civil liberties lawyers would likely express disapproval on fairness grounds: those released early would be being treated better than other offenders receiving similar sentences before or afterwards (presumably the tabloids and the public would find this deficiency less than galvanizing).

The judiciary would be aghast that 'their' sentences were not to be enforced. This is an odd but not uniquely English judicial attitude, that in some non-trivial sense wrongs are being done to judges if the sentences they order are not carried out. This is a nonsense. Sentences are often a measure more of the judges who impose them than of the offenders who receive them. That is a good reason to conclude that judges have no legitimate interest in having their sentences carried out.

Wholesale releases of prisoners for celebratory reasons, or openly and mundanely to reduce prisoner numbers, are unlikely to happen anytime soon in England. In France, it is easy to imagine a Gallic shrug as the commonest reaction to such announcements: 'Bonne chance' or 'C'est la vie'. In England, widespread outrage is likely. Whatever their merits in French eyes, and their acceptability within French penal culture, wholesale releases are not likely to be politically or culturally viable in the English-speaking countries.

* * * *

It wasn't inevitable that English political leaders chose to emulate American models of law-and-order politics and crime-control policy rather than those on offer in Canada or Germany or Sweden or France. In that sense, the runaway prison population, the opportunity costs England pays when it invests in prisons rather than in schools or hospitals, and the exacerbating effects of imprisonment on the social exclusion experienced by disadvantaged people, are simply costs that Labour has been willing to pay to increase its odds of staying in power. The three factors I've highlighted – postmodernist angst aggravated by too much crime prevention, cultural attitudes favouring debasement of prisoners, and the taste for punishment – helped make Labour's political strategy a successful one.

Although prevalent cultural attitudes toward crime and criminals may explain English acceptance of Labour's crime-control policies, that acceptance cannot justify those policies. The Labour government could, as presumably most other European governments have chosen to do, have decided that what is popular, or politically saleable, is not acceptable unless it is also morally right or ethically justifiable. Criminal law and punishment implicate fundamental questions of moral autonomy, social disadvantage, civil liberties, justice and fairness that deserve to be addressed on the substantive merits. This government, and the last of John Major's, appear to have decided that only low visibility and non-contentious issues should be dealt with on their merits, and the visible and contentious ones on how solutions will be seen by tabloid editors and focus-group participants. In the long term those are disastrous bases for policy-making.

Two questions remain. Why did these politicians, and this government, in this time, and this place, play the crime card, and why in a time of falling crime rates do they keep doing it? Those answers are known, if by anyone, only by senior figures in the Labour Party.

Footnote

1 In a foreword to *Adventures in Criminology* (1999), Sir Leon Radzinowicz's final book, Woolf wrote: 'The present Labour government is having to pay for its failure to vigorously oppose the populist penal policies of the previous Conservative government. The sad spectacle of the previous government and the opposition competing for the title of being toughest on crime is now haunting the present government' (1999: xii).

Chapter 4

Race

Race matters, or at least it should. Black people in England and Wales are much more likely than whites or Asians to be arrested and prosecuted for violent and drug crimes, and they are much more likely to be convicted and imprisoned for those crimes. Major assessments of the Metropolitan Police, the Crown Prosecution Service and the Prison Service have described these agencies as institutionally racist, and their senior executives have accepted the description as apt. There is widespread belief among minority communities and their leaders that minority suspects, defendants and offenders are treated unfairly.

For all those reasons, one might expect a comprehensive overhaul of the criminal justice system to contain numerous provisions aimed at improving the experiences of members of minority groups in their dealings with the justice system. Not one provision of the Criminal Justice Act 2003 addresses the subject. This is starkly illustrated by one of the 'frequently asked questions' about the 2003 Act included on a Home Office web page. The question is a good one: 'Is there anything in the Act that will improve the experience of ethnic minorities in the CJS?' The two-sentence reply is a *non sequitur* that ducks the question.

The first sentence: 'We are doing all we can to improve criminal justice services for all people, regardless of ethnic background, age or gender.' In other words, though minority citizens face special problems in their dealings with the criminal justice system, the government has no special plans to address them.

The second sentence: 'Ethnic minorities tend to be based in some of the communities most vulnerable to crime and it is in these communities that the benefits of the proposals in the Act will be felt most keenly.' Communities and citizens generally may or may not benefit from the Act's provisions, but that claim misses the point. It addresses interests of minority citizens as *victims* or potential victims, not as *suspects and offenders*, and it is in the latter capacities that the system is broadly believed to treat minority persons unfairly.

The problems of disparate criminal justice system treatment of black people are enormous. On 30 June 2000, for example, black men constituted 2.4 per cent of the general population of men in England and Wales, and 12 per cent of the male prison population. The difference was even more pronounced for black women: of women in the general population, 2.5 per cent were black; of women in prison, 19 per cent were.

The reality is far worse than the numbers look. One might think that five times more black men are in prison than their presence in the population justifies (dividing 12 per cent by 2.4) and seven-and-a-half times more black women. Those ratios, high though they are, understate the problem. When chances that members of different groups in prison are calculated relative to population, black men in England are seven times more likely than white or Asian men to be in prison, and the differential between black and white and Asian women is worse. English racial disparities in imprisonment are at least as bad as those affecting blacks in the United States.

However calculated, these are disturbing numbers. Black imprisonment rates are a social and public policy problem of the first order. Imprisonment damages people. Current imprisonment practices impose far greater damage on blacks, as a group, than on whites or Asians. Insofar as the Labour government is serious about tackling social exclusion, it should be trying to minimize avoidable harm done by the state to members of visible minority groups.

The government put forward a wide-ranging and ambitious package of proposed changes to the criminal justice system in the White Paper, the Criminal Justice Bill and the Criminal Justice Act. No mention is made of racial disparities in imprisonment as a pressing problem. Among all the major policy documents, the subject is ignored except for a buck-passing mention in the Halliday report. Halliday devoted one paragraph to racial and ethnic dimensions of sentencing policy.

Here word for word are Halliday's three proposals (Home Office 2001b: 16):

> [1] [T]he general principle applying to levels of punishment should be one of equal treatment, regardless of cultural, religious or ethnic background.

[2] [D]iscrimination needs to be tackled across the criminal justice system as a whole, as sentencing outcomes will be necessarily influenced by the types of offenders brought before the courts.

[3] Monitoring outcomes is the key to achieving non-discrimination, and this should involve the systematic collection of data between all criminal justice agencies and appropriate research.

Hardly rousing, or communicating any sense of urgency. It would be unfair, however, to subject Halliday's discussion to close analysis since he clearly didn't see the subject as central to the concerns of his inquiry (though that by itself is interesting).

Two things stand out. First, the problem Halliday identifies is deliberate, ill-motivated, invidious 'discrimination.' I use inverted commas because in 2001 the rest of the criminal justice system – police, prisons, prosecution, probation – was reeling under the pressure of allegations of 'institutional racism'. The latter focuses, as did MacPherson's report on the Metropolitan Police in connection with the Stephen Lawrence case, on processes that 'disadvantage minority ethnic people,' which imprisonment disparities unarguably do.

Second, by ducking the subject, Halliday passed up a wonderful opportunity to focus policy-makers' minds on how current practices unnecessarily disadvantage minority offenders. Many of Halliday's proposals clearly influenced the content of the White Paper and the Criminal Justice Act. A sizeable number of sentencing policies and practices in England should be rethought because of the ways in which they unnecessarily damage minority, especially black, offenders. All can be re-evaluated on their merits. Many should be changed. Had Halliday proposed ways to lessen or ameliorate racial disparities, the government would have been obliged at least to explain why it rejected his proposals.

The two primary strategies now in place in England for addressing racial and ethnic issues in the criminal justice system – attacking institutional racism and sensitizing public employees to cultural and ethic differences – both miss the point when it comes to sentencing and punishment. Once current crimes, past criminal records and case processing differences are taken into account, current research does not suggest that prison disparities are primarily or significantly the result of biased decisions by judges. At the margins, it is likely that stereotypes of minority offenders in the minds of middle- and upper-class judges make them likelier to see minority offenders as dangerous or deserving of severe punishment, but there is no evidence that the effect of this on sentencing disparities is large.

Disparities in imprisonment occur mostly because proportionately more black than white offenders are convicted of the kinds of drug and serious violent crimes that typically result in prison sentences. Courts, of course, can sentence only those offenders brought before them, but in relation to serious violent crimes there is no substantial evidence that prosecutors and police treat whites favourably and blacks unfavourably when they decide whom to arrest or prosecute, or for what. Concerning drug crimes, the picture is a bit more complicated because police disproportionately target drug markets and trafficking in minority areas; however, there is no evidence of substantial racial differences in arresting and prosecuting people once they have been identified as playing major drug-trafficking roles (Bowling and Phillips 2001).

Once suspects have been arrested and prosecuted, however, a number of laws and procedures adversely affect black offenders, even though neither in principle nor by design are they meant to do so. The most prominent is the well-established doctrine that people who plead guilty promptly are entitled to a substantial reduction in sentence, with those who plead guilty later receiving progressively smaller reductions. This policy systematically disadvantages black defendants, as Hood (1992) showed in his ground-breaking research on ethnic differences in sentencing in Midlands courts. Black defendants are less likely than whites to plead guilty and when they do plead guilty, they do so at later stages. The racial difference in pleading guilty results in part from the greater alienation that blacks feel toward a criminal justice system that many believe treats them unfairly.

The circle that closes is a pretty grim one. Young black men are disproportionately stopped by the police and many feel – often no doubt rightly – that they are hassled and stopped under circumstances when young white men, or older black men, would not be. Not surprisingly, many distrust the police and the legal system and, when arrested or charged with a crime, act defiantly and uncooperatively. The criminal justice system lacks legitimacy in their eyes. As a result they do not plead guilty and, because of that, they are punished more severely. Put into a single sentence: young black men who believe themselves unfairly treated by the police understandably become angry and uncooperative, and are punished more severely as a result. Problems of this sort are significant causes of racial disparities in imprisonment in England and Wales, and they must be solved if disparities are to be reduced.

Racial disparities in imprisonment should be viewed as a problem of crisis proportion that warrants emergency responses. Here are seven. First, most importantly, reduce the prison population by one-third. Because blacks are heavily over-represented among prisoners, they would as a group disproportionately benefit from down-sizing the prison population. Second, the Court of Appeal should announce a one-third reduction in sentences specified in all existing guideline judgments. Reduction in sentence lengths is a much more effective way to reduce population than are reductions in prison admissions. Third, policies should be developed to divert large numbers of minor cases from the courts and the prisons. This is not the best way to reduce the size of the prison population, but it is the best way to reduce the number of individuals whose lives are disrupted by imprisonment. Fourth, the existing mandatory minimums for burglaries, violent crimes, drug offences and, under the Criminal Justice Act 2003, firearms offences, should be repealed. Blacks are heavily over-represented among persons in prison for many of these crimes. Fifth, current guilty plea practices that award a substantial sentence reduction to people who plead guilty should be changed. Black defendants less often plead guilty and when they do, they do it later. The discount results in harsher sentences for black offenders as a class. Sixth, racial disparity audits should be carried out throughout the justice system in order to identify practices that disproportionately adversely affect minority offenders; whenever possible those practices should be changed. Pre-trial detention practices are particularly likely targets for improvement. Seventh, Parliament should require that every proposed change to laws affecting sentencing or punishment be accompanied by a minority impact assessment that projects likely effects of proposed changes on all major ethnic groups. If laws are going to be enacted that will worsen disparities, lawmakers should be forced to acknowledge what they are doing and explain why it is justified.

The section below on 'Reducing racial disparities' discusses those proposals in that order. First, I discuss recent, not especially useful, attempts to use the epithet 'institutional racism' as a club with which to beat bureaucracies into ethical behaviour. I discuss the concept not because it has much useful to contribute to efforts to understand or reduce racial disparities in punishment – it doesn't – but because it has received much recent attention, and failure to discuss it might be seen by many as a cardinal oversight. My aim is to explain why the concept sheds little useful light either in general or on punishment in particular.

The term 'institutional racism' is unfortunate – it allows some people to feel sanctimonious and gets other people's backs up – but its initial proponents were not ill-motivated. They were concerned about real and important problems of unconscious attribution and stereotyping, and about cultural insensitivity. Sentencing and punishment disparities will not be much affected if these problems are ameliorated, but they should be attacked in their own right.

'Institutional racism'

Heads of criminal justice agencies in 2001–02 queued up to declare their organizations 'institutionally racist'. Notable declarants include Sir Paul Condon, Commissioner of the Metropolitan Police; David Calvert Smith, Director of Public Prosecutions; and Martin Narey, Director General of the Prison Service. These statements followed Sir William Macpherson's controversial use of the term, in his report on the death of black teenager Stephen Lawrence, to include unwitting discrimination on the part of organizations.

The fundamental problem with terms such as 'institutional racism' is that they are polar words, conversation-stoppers rather than conversation starters. To say that someone or something is racist, fascist, bigoted or homophobic is to accuse them of something hateful. Not surprisingly, people don't like to be accused of acting hatefully, and often they respond by taking offence, stalking away, or vehemently denying the accusation.

Here is how Sir William Macpherson defined the term 'institutional racism' in his report:

> The collective failure of an organization to provide an appropriate and professional service to people because of their colour, culture or ethnic origin. It can be seen or detected in processes, attitudes and behaviour which amount to discrimination through unwitting prejudice, ignorance, thoughtlessness, and racist stereotyping which disadvantage minority ethnic people.
>
> (Macpherson 1999: 321)

That is extraordinarily artless, and almost incoherent. 'Racist stereotyping' surely is *per se* racist; decisions predicated on racist stereotypes are as bad as any other decisions predicated on racist attitudes. The hard problem is stereotyping that, though not ill-motivated, or deliberate, results in different and worse treatment of minority offenders. Likewise, 'unwitting prejudice' is an oxymoron: actions and attitudes that are 'unwitting' can't be the product of prejudice in the pejorative sense. Prejudice is prejudice. Treating people differently because of prejudice is not unwitting: it is prejudicial. Treating people differently unwittingly is not treating them differently because of prejudice.

The structure of Macpherson's key language – '[F]ailure … to provide … appropriate and professional service to people *because of* their colour' (emphasis added) – describes failures based on, resulting from, or motivated by (those synonyms just about exhaust the usual meanings of 'because of') people's colour. That sounds like simple garden-variety racial bias. Macpherson's statement, however, is generally interpreted to refer to 'racism' that is not intentional. Sylvia Denman, in her report on the Crown Prosecution Service, tried to save Macpherson's statement with this gloss: ' "Institutional racism" is unconscious or systemic in nature' (Denman 2001: 93).

That's clearer. It distinguishes the problem being addressed from actions that deliberately or invidiously treat people differently *because of* their race or ethnicity. However, it doesn't explain why the epithet 'racism', rather than, say, insensitivity, is used to describe it. (The reason, of course, is clear: accusations of racism are galvanizing and attract attention; 'institutional insensitivity' or 'racial insensitivity' are much less emotive terms).

Much of the confusion arises from Macpherson's mistaken assumption that racial disparities within the justice system result from two processes: invidious racism by individuals and unintended differences in treatment by organizations. There are, however, three importantly different phenomena to be distinguished: invidiously motivated actions, processes and outcomes that are meant to treat members of minority groups differently; actions, processes and outcomes based on un-conscious racial (not 'racist') stereotypes; and actions, processes and outcomes that are not based on racial stereotypes, and are not undertaken with the intent to treat members of minority groups differently or worse, but systematically do so.

People who toss about the term 'institutional racism' often elide these ethically quite different phenomena, with counterproductive results. Individuals working within institutions tarred with the institutional racism brush feel as if they are being accused of being racists – many people working in police departments, prisons and prosecution offices reacted that way – and categorically deny it. Alternatively, both the blameless and the blameworthy, if they understand the epithet to be no more than a bit of consciousness-raising rhetoric, may feel exonerated because the problem is anonymous and impersonal: in the system, but not in them.

The concept of institutional racism offers no insights or guidance on how to address the major cause of racial differences in sentencing and imprisonment, practices and processes falling into the third category, that are not meant to affect members of minority groups worse, but do. Sentence reductions for guilty pleas are the paradigm case.

Racial disparities arising from the guilty plea discount policy are 'systemic' in nature but that does not make them institutionally or any other kind of racist. The disparities point up a serious policy problem, and throwing the word 'racist' at it does not help solve it. The problem is that undesirable but foreseeable disparities are counterbalanced in many people's minds by the need to encourage guilty pleas and the common belief that sentence discounts are an indispensable means to that end.

Use of polar words that make people defensive is not a good way to start a conversation. A more productive way is to try to reach agreement that a problem exists, to search for evidence of its causes and extent, and then to search for strategies to solve or ameliorate it.

There is little credible evidence that sentencing or imprisonment disparities are solely or largely the product of racial bias or enmity, or ill-will toward minority offenders (Reiner 1992; Smith 1997; Bowling and Phillips 2001). That being so, searching out and removing racist judges and other officials, or eliminating policies that intentionally discriminate, will not do much to reduce disparities. What is needed is a wholesale effort to identify existing practices and policies that adversely affect members of ethnic minority groups and then to consider whether their aims can't be better or equally well realized in other ways.

Reducing racial disparities

So what can be done to reduce disproportionate imprisonment of blacks and related appearances of injustice and race-based illegitimacy in the criminal justice system? This section considers the seven proposals set out earlier in this chapter. All require a bit of political courage from somebody, most often the government. Some relate to sentencing, some to sentencing policy, some to processes and practices that exacerbate disparities, and some to lawmaking.

The most promising approach is to tackle issues openly and honestly, identifying factors that cause or worsen disparities, doing whatever research or inquiry is needed to understand how they operate and why, and then systematically to consider whether policy objectives whose pursuit causes disparities, like the aim of inducing guilty pleas, are more important than the aim of reducing disparities. Some of these discussions will be heated and some acrimonious, but surely it is better to talk them out in public than to allow the issues to fester in the darkness while minority defendants continue to experience unfair treatment.

Reduce the prison population by one-third

England imprisons its black residents at rates about seven times higher than its white residents. Much the most effective way to reduce unnecessary intrusion of imprisonment into black people's lives, however, is not to focus on imprisonment rates and ratios but on the overall use of imprisonment.

No politically saleable reform proposals for tinkering with sentencing criteria will have dramatic effects on racial disparities in imprisonment. If, however, the prison population were reduced by one-third, blacks in absolute terms would benefit greatly. From their perspective as a group, there would be substantially greater benefit if absolute levels of imprisonment were cut by a third (even if the seven-times disproportion continued or even worsened) than if the prison population stayed where it is or went up and the rate of disproportion declined somewhat.

The white incarceration rate, for example, was 170 per 100,000 white British nationals aged 15–64 on 30 June 2001. The black rate was 1,140. That represents a 6.7:1 ratio. Holding the prison population constant while bringing the ratio down 10 per cent to 6:1 would be progress, but in terms of human lives blighted by imprisonment it would constitute much less progress than reducing the prison population by a third while retaining the 6.7:1 ratio.

Table 4.1 shows the hypothetical numbers. If the ratio were reduced from 6.7:1 to 6:1, but the prison population remained the same, the black imprisonment rate would fall by 80 per 100,000 people, and the white rate would increase by five. If the ratio remained the same, but the number of prisoners were reduced by one-third, the black imprisonment rate would fall by 376 per 100,000, and the white rate by 56. Relative to population, four-and-a-half times more blacks would be spared imprisonment if the total prison population were cut than if the ratio of disproportion were reduced.

The calculation just described is simple and assumes that numbers could be reduced across the board. In real life it would be more complicated. A sophisticated prediction of the effects of such a

Table 4.1 Hypothetical disparities in incarceration rates by ethnicity

	Black	White	Ratio
Imprisonment rate, 30 June 2001	1140	170	6.7:1
Imprisonment rate if less disparity	1060	175	6:1
Change in rate per 100,000	–80	+5	
Imprisonment rate	1140	170	6.7:1
Imprisonment reduced by one-third	764	114	6.7:1
Reduction in rate per 100,000	–376	–56	

Source: Home Office 2003.
Note: Imprisonment rates per 100,000 residents aged 15–64

reduction would have to take into account the offences of which members of different groups are convicted and the lengths of the terms they serve. Black offenders are disproportionately convicted of drug and violent offences, for which sentences are imposed that are longer than the overall mean. As a result, the decrease in the black incarceration rate resulting from a one-third reduction in the size of the prison population might be somewhat less than I have estimated. It would, however, be very substantial.

The proposal raises three important sets of policy issues: costs, international comparisons and crime-prevention effects. First consider costs. Confining one prisoner for one year in an English prison costs £36,000 (Home Office 2003). As I write, Her Majesty's prisons hold about 75,000 people. Reducing the population to 50,000 would save £900 million per year. This might be thought of as a 'release dividend.' Of course, it couldn't be done all at once, so the full annual savings would not be realized until the change was fully phased in. Nearly nine hundred million per year is not a small sum to be freed up for other uses, some within the prison and probation systems.

The resulting imprisonment rate of 85–95 per 100,000 population would then be ordinary by European standards – a bit higher than those in Scandinavia and about the same as those in France, Germany and Italy, the other most populated countries in the EU. English crime rates and recent crime trends fall within normal patterns for large countries, so there's no obvious reason why English imprisonment rates should be the highest of the large European countries.

Now consider crime prevention. Though this may seem counter-intuitive, reducing the prison population by a third should bring crime rates down. There are several reasons for this. First, recidivism studies comparing re-offending by people released from prisons or community penalties generally conclude that ex-prisoners do worse and have higher re-offending rates. They certainly do not do better. The Halliday report conservatively concluded, '[T]here is currently no discernible difference between reconviction rates for custody and for community penalties' (Home Office 2001b: 126). Since the eighteenth-century times of John Howard, critics have characterized prisons as schools for crime in which offenders become more deeply socialized into criminal values and from which they are released stigmatized as 'ex-cons'. This is why several countries, including Germany, have nearly eliminated the use of prison sentences of six months or less (Weigend 2001). They are seen as too short to allow rehabilitative programmes to be effective, but long enough for prisoners to lose their jobs, their homes and their families. So reducing the prison population will not result in more crimes by people who've completed their sentences, and will lessen prisons' criminogenic effects.

Second, deterrence. Although some people, including many judges, believe that harsher penalties have greater deterrent effects than milder ones, there is no evidence that this is true. To the contrary, every serious review of research in the past quarter century on the deterrent effects of punishment has concluded that there is no evidence to support the belief that incremental differences in punishment have measurable deterrent effects (von Hirsch *et al.* 1999; Blumstein *et al.* 1978; Reiss and Roth 1993; Cook 1980; Nagin 1998; Doob and Webster 2003). Here is what Halliday said, '[T]here seems to be no link between marginal changes in punishment levels and changes in crime rates ... It is the prospect of getting caught that has deterrence value, rather than alterations to the "going rate" for severity of sentences' (Home Office 2001b: 8). So, there is no reason to believe that reducing the length of every prison sentence pro rata would result in any lesser deterrent effects than retaining them at their current levels.

Third, treatment programmes. Reducing the prison population by a third will enable substantial improvements in the quality and availability of treatment programmes in the prison and in the community. Though substantial evidence has accumulated that well-managed, well-targeted programmes can reduce participants' later offending, sufficient funds are seldom available to allow adequate implementation and to meet the needs of eligible offenders (Gaes *et al.* 1999; US Surgeon General 2001). Limited availability, poor targeting and inadequate aftercare in drug-abuse treatment, for example, are commonly recognized to be serious problems, as is attested by scathing reports by

H.M. Inspector of Prisons on Wandsworth and Liverpool prisons in May and June 2003.

Even a third of the £900 million release dividend will go a long way to meet treatment needs in prisons and the community. In addition, reduction in prison populations will allow prison governors to devote more facilities, staff time and money to treatment programmes than current overcrowding permits. If treatment programmes can reduce re-offending – and the evidence is that they can – the release dividend will permit substantial crime prevention gains.

The only substantive argument against a one-third reduction in the prison population is that doing so would sacrifice some of the incapacitative effects of current imprisonment levels. This is true. It must be weighed, however, against the social inclusion gains from doing less damage to members of England's black disadvantaged population, the £900 million per year that could be saved, and the reductions in crime that would be achieved through substantially greater investment in treatment programming. Econometric modellers can and should begin work to help policy-makers understand better the trade-offs between current and radically altered imprisonment practices and levels.

In any event, though arguments about incapacitation and averted serious crimes can be emotionally powerful, they face a diminishing-returns problem. No doubt, for example, a doubling of the current imprisonment rate would avoid some crimes through incapacitation. If that were to be proposed today though, discussions would inevitably take place about cost-effectiveness (how much would it cost per avoided crime and is that more or less than other crime-prevention approaches?), opportunity costs (would the additional money be better spent on prisons or schools or health care or the military?), and intrusions on liberty (would the aggregate additional crime prevention achieved justify the aggregate additional deprivations of people's liberty?). My guess is that a proposal to double current numbers would be rejected as too expensive and as undesirable on the merits, even though some crimes might be prevented.

In thinking about the desirability of cutting current numbers by one-third, it would be wise to perform a thought experiment and imagine that the numbers are a third lower and that what must be decided is whether to increase them by half. In other words, think back a few years to when the prison population was about 48,000 and consider whether a substantial increase would be a good idea and worth the money. Here too, my guess is that the answer then, had the question been posed in that way, would have been 'No'. If that's so, a current one-third reduction would be no more than a correction of an undesirable and unintended shift in practice that produced an unwanted result.

The arguments in favour of a reduction in prison use are powerful. How should it be effected? A one-time set of across-the-board early releases on licence would bring the population down. To keep it down, the principal methods available are to send fewer people to prison, to reduce sentence lengths, or to do both. Reductions in sentence lengths would be the more effective, so I start there, though a reduction strategy should incorporate both reductions in committals to prisons and in sentence lengths.

Reduce guideline judgement sentence prescriptions by a third

The Court of Appeal's guideline judgements provide a ready tool for reducing the lengths of prison sentences – reduce the sentence lengths prescribed by one-third across the board. There is no credible evidence to suggest that the criminal law's deterrent effects would thereby be undermined. Certainty of punishment will be unaffected and all the available evidence suggests that changes in times served from 15 to 10 months or from 60 to 40 will have no impact on punishment's deterrent effects.

An across-the-board reduction will also preserve the punishment system's moral-educative effects. Scandinavian scholars for many years have argued that punishment's most powerful effects are not through deterrence, incapacitation or rehabilitation but through the ways the criminal law does or does not reiterate and reinforce basic social norms and values (e.g., Andenaes 1974). For the most part, the Scandinavians argue, people do or do not commit crimes because of the kind of people they are, and that is determined by their socialization into positive values. Primary socialization occurs, however, in families and schools and neighbourhoods, not in courts and prisons. The criminal justice system can reinforce or undermine social values but it cannot itself do the heavy lifting. Therefore it is highly important that bad actions have consequences. For this reason, the likelihood that offenders receive prison or equivalent sentences in Finland and Sweden is higher than it is in England and America (Kommer 1994). For this reason also, however, Scandinavian prison sentences are typically much shorter than in England or America. If there's no reason to believe that lengths of sentence affect deterrent effects, and if short but proportionate sentences support social norms, there's nothing to be gained from long sentences (Jareborg 1995; Lappi-Seppälä 2001).

This analysis assumes that trial judges follow guidelines judgements and will adjust their sentencing behaviour in light of reductions. Little good empirical evidence is available on how judges respond to guideline judgements (Wasik 2001), but it seems odd to assume that judges will ignore authoritative pronouncements of the Court of Appeal.

Sentences could be reduced in other ways of course – selectively offence-by-offence, for example – or by another means. The Criminal Justice Act creates a Sentencing Council charged to promulgate guideline judgements. For reasons given in Chapter 5, I'm exceedingly doubtful that what has been proposed can work, but no matter. The important thing is not which body reduces the lengths of prison sentences but that they be reduced.

A weakness of existing guideline judgements may for purposes of prison population reduction be a strength. Commentators such as Ashworth (2001) have criticized the judgements for their limited scope. They deal mostly with serious offences and have not been adequately developed for the less serious, high-volume crimes that provide most of the courts' business. This may be an advantage from a prison-reduction perspective. Crimes not serious enough to be the subjects of guidelines judgements are obvious candidates for diversion from prison altogether.

Divert minor cases from the courts and prisons

Reducing the size of the prison population will depend most critically on shortening medium-length and long sentences. One prisoner serving five years takes up as many prison beds as 30 prisoners serving two months each. Self-evidently, space will much more easily be saved by reducing longer sentences.

Nonetheless, part of the effort must involve diverting people from prison. This can be done in three ways: sentence to community penalties some categories of offenders now sent to prison; devise ways to get some people now in prisons out earlier; reduce the use of confinement as a penalty for breaches of conditions.

Plenty of room exists for placing more people who now receive prison sentences into community programmes. The 'What works' initiatives provide numerous programme models for adoption. The Criminal Justice Act's custody-plus and suspended sentence provisions are both premised on such programmes' presumed capacity to reduce reoffending rates.

In addition, new systems of prosecutorial diversion patterned on Dutch 'transactions' and German 'conditional dismissals' would enable large numbers of offenders to be diverted from the courts. English magistrates and judges have a taste for custody, so keeping cases away from them by definition will reduce prison use. In the Dutch and German programmes, defendants are offered the opportunity to pay or perform the penalty that would be imposed had they been convicted, usually unit fines, community service or restitution, in exchange for dismissal of the charges against them. The defendant need not plead guilty and the charges will not be revived if the agreed penalty is performed (Tak 2001; Weigend 2001).

Another approach is to give incentives to sentencers to divert cases. There are enormous variations among magistrates' courts in sentencing of minor cases such as shop-lifting, driving under suspension and simple assault. This necessarily means that many of those sentences are being imposed idiosyncratically or capriciously, for reasons that have more to do with the magistrate than the offender. The Metropolitan Police recently floated but quickly abandoned a proposal to give £300 bonuses to minority officers for each minority person they recruited to enter the police service. Whatever the idea's demerits for police recruitment, it has much to commend it for magistrate motivation.

Suppose sentencers were told that a £300 contribution would be made to any licensed charity of their choice for each offender in a defined category whom they sentenced to a community punishment? From a public safety or a crime-prevention perspective it can't make the slightest difference whether 20 per cent or 80 per cent of driving-while-suspended offenders receive gaol terms, so successful diversion of many more than at present would be an unqualifiedly good thing. And when the £300 bonus is compared with the costs of imprisoning a single offender for a week or a few months, the public savings would be enormous.

At the back-end of the system, programme models are available for getting people out of prison early. Among the most promising is the Dutch system of 'penitentiary sanctions.' The Dutch Prison Service is authorized to release prisoners early into any of a wide range of community programmes. The particular programme is selected on the basis of diagnoses of the individual's risks and needs and enables the application of 'What works' learning on a case-by-case basis (Tak 2001). Home detention curfew is a narrow English equivalent that could be expanded greatly.

Finally, offenders can be 'diverted' in one more sense by reducing the pressures for and incidence of imprisonment of offenders following breaches of conditions. Both Jack Straw, in relation to home detention curfew, and David Blunkett, in relation to custody-minus, trumpeted their insistence on near-automatic incarceration of people who violate conditions of community penalties. People violate conditions for all sorts of reasons and sensible policies would call for individualized consideration of how violations should be dealt with. Ham-fisted policies of automatic incarceration produce unjust and inappropriate responses and send too many people to prison.

Repeal all mandatory minimum sentence laws

Mandatory minimum sentence laws are simply bad public policy. Their defects are well known. They cause undue rigidities which sometimes result in manifestly unjust penalties in individual cases, and in other cases they result in hypocritical efforts of judges and lawyers to circumvent their application. The resulting arbitrariness sometimes produces stark disparities in handling of comparable cases. The arbitrariness also undermines perceptions of the law's legitimacy in the eyes of offenders and observers. And there is no evidence that implementation of such laws has any deterrent effects. The injustices they cause are offset by no arguable compensating gains (Tonry 1996: chap. 5).

Mandatories prescribe unusually long sentences – sometimes life – for offences to which they apply, and do particular damage to minority offenders. In England, the principal mandatories affect murder, violent crimes including robbery, burglary, drug offences, and, under the Criminal Justice Act, firearms offences. The problem is that, relative to population, blacks much more often than whites receive prison sentences for many such crimes. In 1999/2000, blacks made up less than 3 per cent of the English population. Among prisoners, however, blacks made up 18 per cent of those committed for violence against the person, 21 per cent of robbers, 10 per cent of burglars, and 28 per cent of drug offenders (Home Office 2000: 45). All those numbers are heavily disproportionate to blacks' presence in the population – the robbery and drugs numbers stunningly so. Special laws requiring especially long sentences for those crimes by definition impose special burdens of imprisonment on black people, and related undesirable collateral effects on prisoners' families and communities.

On that ground alone, they should be repealed. As a matter of evidence-based policy-making, they should be repealed. As part of a comprehensive strategy to reduce the prison population, they must be repealed. If guideline judgement prescriptions were reduced by a third, mandatory minimums would trump any inconsistent guideline-sentence judgement, and for that reason should be repealed.

Abandon sentence discounts for guilty pleas

This point was made in the introduction to this chapter. This policy, which may or may not exemplify 'institutional racism', produces longer sentences for black offenders than for whites because black offenders plead guilty less often and typically later in the process. Those longer sentences cannot be justified as a matter of social policy even though they have long been deemed justifiable as a matter of criminal justice policy.

Judges assume that the courts will grind to a halt if defendants are not offered substantial incentives to plead guilty, but there is little evidence that this is true. The limited amount of evidence from American plea-bargaining bans suggests that most defendants plead guilty even when they are not offered sentencing concessions (Blumstein *et al.* 1983, chap. 3). In any event, analysis of the subject would force officials to develop estimates of the cost savings associated with discount practices, and of the amount of increased imprisonment that blacks in England suffer as a result. Whether measurable cost savings that the discount achieves justify the increased racial imprisonment disparities they cause is a question to which reasonable people might offer different answers. It should be openly discussed and answered.

Carry out racial disparity audits throughout the justice system

This is the preceding proposal writ large, and applies to a wide variety of practices that are facially neutral but have racially disparate effects. By 'facially neutral,' I mean things like the guilty plea discount. In the abstract, or in principle, it has nothing to do with race. The people who developed it over time were presumably entirely indifferent to the identities or ethnicities of the offenders it affected. Their interests were in saving time, bother and expense by giving offenders incentives to plead guilty and to acknowledge the contrition that confessions sometimes are said to express.

By 'disparate impact,' I refer to disproportionate effects on, or burdens borne by, minority groups as a result of operation of a particular policy. In practice, the guilty plea discount produces harsher punishments for black offenders. No one would disagree that it would be unacceptable if it had been designed to disadvantage black offenders. Now that we know it does harm them, is it any less objectionable?

Lots of routine 'facially neutral' criminal justice practices other than the guilty plea discount adversely affect minority offenders. One way to address them is to subject all criminal justice system practices to disparity audits to establish whether and to what extent they exacerbate or ameliorate disparities in outcomes affecting members of minority groups.

Pre-trial detention is a notorious example. Blacks make up an even larger disproportion of the remand population (17 per cent) in England than of the sentenced offender population (13 per cent) (Home Office 2003: 111). In most Western countries, including England (Hood 1992; Smith 1997), minority offenders are doubly disadvantaged by pre-trial detention. First, all else being equal, they are more likely to be held in gaol before trial than are white defendants. Second, all else being equal, people held in gaol before trial receive harsher sentences if convicted than people who were at liberty before trial (Tonry 1997: 16).

The first of these racial disparities occurs because decisions about pre-trial detention often take account of social factors such as the defendant's educational background, vocational skills, residential stability or family status. These are not nonsensical factors. The key issue is whether the defendant will appear for trial or run away, and indicators of social instability and weak local connections are plausible criteria for predicting that the defendant will not appear. Unfortunately, relatively more blacks in England than whites are poor and socially disadvantaged. They will be less likely to benefit from the positive social factors and more likely to be held in gaol pending trial.

Why offenders detained before trial receive longer sentences is less clear, though that pattern has been documented in a number of countries. Perhaps judges in setting sentences take the same social factors that influenced the remand decision into account and on their basis decide that detained offenders are more dangerous or more antisocial. Perhaps judges have a gestalt sense that an earlier judge must have thought the detained offender especially undeserving or dangerous and are influenced by the earlier judge's presumed assessment. Or maybe, because the detained offender's work and family relations have already been disrupted by gaol, judges may be less worried about the harm a prison sentence might cause. Whatever the reasons, the pattern exists and it harms minority offenders.

Happily, once the racially disparate impacts of facially neutral pre-trial detention practices are recognized, they can be reduced. The solution is simply to forbid judges to take social factors into account in making pre-trial detention decisions. Other factors related solely to current or past criminality provide nearly as good predictions of appearance at trial, and though they too will be racially skewed, the racial skew will be much less.

Require racial disparity impact assessments for all proposed sentencing laws

This extends the previous proposal for disparate-impact audits of existing practices to cover all proposed statutory or administrative changes affecting sentencing or criminal punishment. If policy-makers were required to acknowledge racial disparities that proposed bills would predictably produce, and justify them in open debate, fewer that worsen disparities would be passed.

However one analyses or judges the ethical dimensions of decisions to continue practices known to disadvantage members of particular ethnic or racial groups, the problems are even greater when new legislation is under consideration. For many purposes in the criminal law, actions taken with knowledge that a particular harmful result is practically certain are treated as being culpably equivalent to actions taken with the intention to produce that harm. Stated more succinctly, purpose and knowledge are often regarded as equally culpable states of mind. In this light, enactment of a law known to be likely to cause racial disparities in punishment could be regarded as ethically equivalent to enactment of a law intended to achieve such disparities.

A clear example is provided by a notorious American federal law, known as the '100-to-1 rule', that punishes sale of five grams of crack cocaine as harshly as the sale of 500 grams of powder cocaine. It is facially neutral. However, because poor blacks typically sell small amounts of crack and whites typically sell powder in varying quantities, in practice the distinction produces much longer sentences for black than for white drug dealers and worsens racial disparities in imprisonment. This law is the single most important cause of racial disparities in imprisonment in the US federal prison system (McDonald and Carlson 1993).

If disparate impact projections and analyses were an obligatory part of the American federal legislative process, policy-makers would have had explicitly to weigh wanted crime-prevention effects against presumably unwanted but foreseeable disparate impacts on black defendants. This would have forced realistic assessments to be made of what preventive effects were likely and how confidently they could be expected to occur. Perhaps after such deliberations, Congress might still have enacted the 100-to-1 rule, but then the decision would explicitly have been made that the likely gains outweighed the undesirable side-effects. Or, the likely drug-abuse reduction gains might have been deemed so speculative that they did not justify the disparate effects at all. Or even, possibly, the decision might have been made that, given a choice between higher drug abuse or crime rates and worsened racial disparities, the latter was the greater evil and the rule should not be adopted. Such analyses would force explicit choices to be made between crime-control policy goals, whether expressive or substantive, and race-relations goals.

Here is an English example. I presented data above showing that 18 per cent of prisoners held in English prisons in 1999/2000 for violence against the person were black, as were 21 per cent of robbers, 10 per cent of burglars, and 28 per cent of drug offenders (Home Office 2000: 45). The arrest data are less extreme but still show substantial disparities. In 1999/2000, 28.2 per cent of persons arrested for robbery were black, as were 7.2 per cent of other violence arrestees, 6 per cent of burglary arrestees, and 9.2 per cent of drug arrestees. All those numbers are vastly disproportionate to the black presence of less than 3 per cent in the general population.

I don't know whether data like these were presented and discussed in Parliament during consideration of the laws that mandate minimum sentences for certain burglaries, violent crimes and drug crimes. They should have been.

Assume for purposes of argument that arrest percentages are an accurate indicator of racial patterns of serious violent crime (the best evidence is that for serious violent crime, arrest proportions are reasonably valid indicators). It is foreseeable that a mandatory minimum for violent crimes will disproportionately affect black offenders. Over time, racial disparities in prisons would foreseeably worsen (as they have) as a result following enactment of the minimum sentence law. Is that a good thing or a bad thing?

Preventing crime is a good thing, but so is preventing racial disparities. If we knew that the increased lengths of sentence would through deterrence and incapacitation decrease the robbery rate by x per cent, for example, or save the lives of y plus or minus ten people, the trade-off could sensibly be discussed. Does an estimated crime-reduction effect of a particular amount justify an increase from, say, 12 to 15 per cent of the prison population who are black? What if no crime reduction effect could credibly be estimated? Could any increase in racial disproportions be justified, or any increase in penalties that would disproportionately affect blacks?

Comparable analyses of projected effects of alternative public policy choices are commonplace (Cook and Ludwig 2001). Planners explicitly weigh estimates of lost life against cost in building roads or designing aircraft. No action can be made perfectly safe and cost inevitably is a consideration. If all cars were design-limited to ten miles an hour and built with heavy steel bodies, we would have many fewer traffic fatalities and injuries. Decisions to make cars faster, lighter and cheaper produce higher projected rates of injury and death and higher medical care costs. The trade-offs are explicitly discussed. Similar trade-offs should be discussed, and explicit choices made, in relation to race and sentencing.

Implementing the last two proposals will not be easy, but they are necessary if England is to reduce the over-representation of blacks in prison. The necessary research and statistical analyses will not be difficult. The pre-trial detention illustration given above is uncomplicated. Once the problem is recognized, criteria that do not treat groups of offenders differently, or that reduce the extent of differential treatment, can be substituted. More difficult are instances like the American 100-to-1 rule where the goal, to try to reduce the direct and indirect effects of drug trafficking, seems desirable but the effect, treating black defendants much more harshly than whites, does not. Among the choices are to accept the unwanted racial disparity, to abandon the drug policy goal, or to compromise. My guess is that that compromise is what would have happened had the choices been more starkly presented. Black crack defendants would still have been sentenced more harshly than white powder defendants, but the differential and the resulting racial disparities would have been less. That would have been a small victory, but a victory all the same.

And so it might have been had English policy-makers been required openly and accountably to discuss trade-offs between projected crime-reductive effects of mandatory minimum sentence laws and foreseeable worsening of racial disparities in English prisons.

Imprisonment harms people and simultaneously through incapacitation reduces and through prisonisation and stigmatisation causes crime. Racial disparities harm members of minority groups directly, and indirectly harm their loved ones, families and communities. Allowing avoidable racial disparities in imprisonment to continue undermines the battle against social exclusion, undermines the legal system's legitimacy in the eyes of minority group members, and morally impoverishes England and Wales. Things need not be as bad as they are.

Chapter 5

Sentencing

The government for all practical purposes abandoned the comprehensive sentencing guidelines that were the centrepiece of John Halliday's recommendations. There appear to be three reasons for this. First, Halliday was concerned about fairness to offenders and consistency in application of the new penalties he proposed, and saw guidelines as an essential tool for furthering those aims. The government does not appear much to care about fairness to offenders.

Second, the English judiciary is notoriously jealous of its discretion over sentencing. Though as a political and constitutional matter the government is entitled to impose its policy preferences on the judiciary, it is apparently unwilling to spend significant political capital in doing so on this subject. This is in stark contrast to its sustained willingness to expend capital over the issue of the Home Secretary's authority, and in the Criminal Justice Act 2003, the Parliament's authority, to set release dates for life-sentenced and notorious prisoners, an issue it does care about.

Third, assuming for the sake of argument that the government cared about fairness and consistency in sentencing, it grossly underestimated the complexity and difficulty of what's involved in developing comprehensive guidelines. The sentencing council/sentencing guidelines scheme enacted will fail to achieve its ostensible aims.

Halliday's core recommendation, the condition precedent, he insisted, to successful implementation of all the other recommendations, was the development of a system of sentencing guidelines that would provide a framework on which all the other major proposals would be hung – a single community punishment order, 'custody-plus' (a combined imprisonment and community sentence), elimination of three- to six-month prison stays, reconfigured prison sentences, and special provisions for dangerous offenders. '[N]ew guidelines for the use of judicial discretion', Halliday wrote, 'will be an essential part of the new framework' (Home Office 2001b: viii). Because his proposals would radically change English sentencing policies, processes and practices, guidelines would be necessary, he said, to assure consistent application of the new system and avoid gross disparities. The need is even greater under the Criminal Justice Act 2003, which enacted all of Halliday's proposed sentencing options and, in suspended sentences and intermittent custody, two more besides.

The need for sentencing guidelines, however, won't go away. The evidence that English sentencing is riddled with unwarranted and therefore unjust disparities in the sentencing of similar cases is overwhelming. Despite the existence and gradual elaboration of guideline judgements for sentencing issued by the Court of Appeal, Martin Wasik, chairman of the Sentencing Advisory Panel, has pointed out, 'There is little or no research evidence of their effectiveness in enhancing consistency' (Wasik 2001: 3).

There is even less reason to be sanguine about consistency in Magistrates' Courts. Halliday showed that the percentage of household burglars sentenced to immediate custody in 1998 ranged from 5.9 per cent to 69.6 per cent in various courts, with custody percentages for other offences ranging from zero to 66.7 for assaults causing actual bodily harm and from 11.8 to 82.7 for driving while disqualified (Home Office 2001b: app. 2, table 6). Some of those differences may result from differences in the kinds of cases particular courts handle, but that can at most be only a small part of the explanation.

Gross disparities are inevitable under existing sentencing laws. England's judicial culture is notoriously hubristic. Current processes celebrate the discretion of individual judges and magistrates. Strong-minded individuals inevitably have a wide range of views about emotive subjects, such as what punishments offenders deserve. Sentences as a result often indicate more about the views and personality of the judge than about the details of the crime or the circumstances of the criminal.

Concern about disparities is not the only reason why Halliday's guidelines proposal was a good one. Even if policy-makers cared not a whit about fairness to offenders, they do care about money and should care about excessive use of imprisonment. They should also care about the overcrowding, deteriorating conditions and increased suicide rates that excessive use of imprisonment has produced.

Guidelines are the only proven mechanism available for structuring judges' discretion and thereby making their sentencing decisions predictable. Only if sentences become predictable can policy-makers know how many prison beds and probation slots will be needed, and when, and how many probation and prison officers. And, conversely, only if discretion is meaningfully structured can policy-makers who do not wish to spend more taxpayers' money on prisons have the option to change sentencing policies instead, with some confidence that judges and magistrates will follow suit.

The Halliday report was the high point for prospects for sentencing guidelines in England and Wales. Halliday's guidelines were to be comprehensive, covering all offences in all Magistrates' and higher courts, and very detailed, including criteria for community penalties and for taking account of prior convictions. They would be orders of magnitude more comprehensive and detailed than existing guideline judgements issued by the Court of Appeal or than existing voluntary guidelines for Magistrates' courts.

Halliday saw a need for guidelines but also realized that much more work than he had been able to do would have to be invested to figure out how they might be developed and what they might look like. It's been downhill since then.

The White Paper, in vague and exiguous terms, described a sentencing council and guidelines, but proposed just about the weakest possible version of the former and obscured the latter by implying that they might be little more than piecemeal additions to existing guideline judgements. The Criminal Justice Bill further diluted Halliday's proposals by putting the council firmly and solely in the hands of the judiciary, dividing responsibility for guidelines among the council, the Sentencing Advisory Panel and the Court of Appeal. The Bill also, rather than charge the council to develop Halliday's comprehensive guidelines, provided merely that, 'The Council may from time to time consider whether to frame sentencing guidelines …'. The Act closely followed the Bill. Very little of Halliday's guideline proposal is left.

The relevant provisions of the Criminal Justice Act 2003 cannot work. The Sentencing Council will be chaired by the Lord Chief Justice and contain 11 other members, of whom seven must be judges and magistrates and the remaining four, though appointed by the Home Secretary, must be vetted by the senior judiciary. The council is not directed, but merely empowered, to promulgate guidelines. Those guidelines need not be comprehensive as Halliday insisted but may be 'general in nature or limited to a particular category of offence or offender' (section 170[1]). The existing Court of Appeal guideline judgements are not repealed or explicitly addressed at all and the existing Sentencing Advisory Panel is not abolished. It will remain in the guidelines business and at any time may propose that the council frame or revise guidelines.

However. It is just barely possible that the government, or some of its members and civil servants, do want to establish meaningful guidelines but have decided that, because of the power and truculence of the judiciary, this can be done only by stealth.

Here is the fairly Byzantine scenario: the council is not required to develop comprehensive guidelines but has power to do so. Both the Home Secretary and the Sentencing Advisory Panel are authorized to propose that guidelines be framed for particular categories of offences or offenders, and the council must consider those proposals. Lord Woolf, the current Lord Chief Justice, presides over the Court of Appeal and the council and has a consultative role in appointment of council members. Should Lord Woolf favour comprehensive guidelines, he could with some help steer the way to their development. If the Home Secretary, the Sentencing Advisory Panel or both proposed development of guidelines for so many categories of offences and offenders as in effect to call for comprehensive guidelines, Lord Woolf could lead the council in consideration and acceptance of such proposals and then lead the programme of development. Wearing his Court of Appeal hat, Lord Woolf could then persuade the Court to accept abrogation of its existing guideline judgements, to be replaced by the new guidelines, and could then rally judicial support for the new guidelines.

The preceding scenario, while technically possible under the provisions of the Criminal Justice Act 2003, involves heroic assumptions and places enormous *ad hominem* reliance on the current wearer of the Lord Chief Justice's robes. Should he sicken or die or retire, it is not likely that his successor will have similar reformist credentials or accomplishments. Nonetheless, in the third section of this chapter, I assume the reform-by-stealth hypothesis, and discuss a range of issues the developers of comprehensive guidelines must address. In the first two sections, I discuss the provisions of the Act in their own terms. Since the treatments of the sentencing council and guidelines in the White Paper, the Bill and the Act are half-hearted and perfunctory, the first section sketches out Halliday's proposals and aims in some detail. The following section canvasses issues concerning the nature, composition, leadership and functions of a sentencing commission, and shows why the arrangements envisioned by the Act are unlikely to work.

What Halliday proposed

Halliday proposed the creation of a sentencing council charged to establish guidelines that would provide presumptive starting points for judicial consideration of sentences in individual cases. His other major recommendations for community, 'custody-plus', and custodial sentences, and his proposals concerning criminal histories and assessments of offenders' needs and risks of re-offending, were all premised on the existence of more detailed and comprehensive guidelines than now exist.

Halliday also urged that guidelines were essential if English sentencing were to be made more consistent and principled. Halliday portrayed 'inconsistency' as the first among a series of limitations of current practice. A natural question is, 'Inconsistency in relation to what?' The Criminal Justice Act 1991 provided a just-deserts answer – inconsistent in relation to the seriousness of the offence of conviction. Punishments should be commensurate with the seriousness of the offence.

Halliday offered a slightly different, 'limited retributivism' answer (Home Office 2001b: app. 8). The seriousness of the offence should be the primary consideration, and should be seen as setting upper and lower bounds of deserved, and thus not unjust, punishments. Within those bounds, a variety of considerations might justify different sentences. Those bounds, however, for Halliday set real limits on what could be done to offenders. Guidelines would take those bounds into account, thereby improving consistency and lessening instances of injustice.

Halliday's guidelines would, for England and Wales, have been unprecedented in scope, complexity and specificity. He stressed that the guidelines must be comprehensive and apply to all courts, if other proposed changes were to have any hope of working. The guidelines would 'specify graded levels of seriousness of offence, presumptive "entry points" of sentence severity in relation to each level of severity, how severity of sentence should increase in relation to numbers and types of prior conviction, and other possible grounds for aggravation and mitigation' (Home Office 2001b: p. viii).

Halliday's guidelines would address all offences, not just a handful of the most serious, including high-volume offences of low and moderate severity for which no guidelines now exist. Existing guideline judgments, by contrast, 'remain clustered around the serious offences that attract substantial prison sentences' and in 2001 did not address the high-volume offences, 'notably burglary, theft, deception, and handling stolen goods,' that constitute the courts' main business (Ashworth 2001: 75).

English policy-makers have not before had to wrestle with top-down formulation of comprehensive, detailed sentencing policies. Parliamentary consideration of proposed changes to criminal and sentencing statutes is top-down but is necessarily pitched at high levels of abstraction and generality. The work of the Court of Appeal is squarely within the common law tradition of iterative development and refinement of doctrine as cases arise. Guideline judgements can be detailed but are not comprehensive across offences and are generally not comprehensive within a single offence. The work of the Sentencing Advisory Panel is potentially comprehensive within single offences but, because it is meant to elaborate and support the Court of Appeal's Common Law methodology, not across offences.

The Magistrates' Courts since the 1960s have been working with voluntary guidelines for some, initially motoring, offences, according to Ashworth (2000: 55):

> [M]agistrates in many areas have been using these [guidelines'] starting points, but in some areas the guidelines have been 'adapted to local conditions' and in a few areas the guidelines are not adopted ... Important as the guidelines may be in offering practical guidance where Parliament and the Court of Appeal are silent, they have no authority whatsoever. They cannot bind magistrates in law, and justices' clerks are aware of this.

Likewise, England has little experience with 'independent bodies' or 'independent judicial bodies' charged to set sentencing policy. The Sentencing Advisory Panel established under sections 80–81 of the Crime and Disorder Act 1998 is the closest England has come to a sentencing council. Its original authority, however, was limited to provision of recommendations to the Court of Appeal about guidelines for particular categories of offences.

The Criminal Justice Act's provisions, as noted above, bear little resemblance to Halliday's proposals. The White Paper paid lip service, proposing '... a consistent set of guidelines that cover all offences and should be applied whenever a sentence is passed' (Home Office 2002a: 89). However, a later passage made it clear that the process envisaged is one of incremental additions to the body of existing guideline judgments, with 'individual guidelines being issued to judges and magistrates ... as and when they are completed' (Home Office 2002a:

90), and the Bill and Act contemplate only such guidelines, of whatever breadth, as the council from time to time chooses to address.

The Criminal Justice Act 2003 on its face

The ample American experience with sentencing councils demonstrates that councils composed solely of judges invariably fail to produce guidelines that significantly restrain the discretion of individual judges. Partly this is because judges are not policy-makers and are unaccustomed to participating in administrative rule-making (which is what guideline drafting is). Mostly, however, it is because judges typically oppose meaningful guidelines in principle, believing strongly that judges should be given wide discretion in setting sentences.

Many statements by many judges could be adduced to demonstrate the typical judicial attitude in Britain. Here's one: in a speech to the Scottish Law Society on 21 March 1993, commenting on early proposals for establishment of a sentencing council, Lord Taylor made the judicial position clear: judges need 'to have available the widest range of measures, and the broadest discretion to deploy them either individually or in combination ... The best approach to sound sentencing is to leave it to the judiciary to exercise their experience and judgement' (quoted in Dunbar and Langdon 1998: 106).

To like effect, I quoted in some detail in an earlier chapter from Hilary Benn's summary of the results from a 2003 consultation exercise on sentencing. He observed that 'It is striking that while most of those observing the sentencers feel that too much use is being made of custody, the sentencers themselves support the current balance between custodial and non-custodial penalties' (Benn 2003: 8).

The nature of the involvement of the judiciary is the single most important element in whether sentencing councils and guidelines succeed or fail. If judges dominate the council's work, it will fail. If judges actively or passively resist guidelines, they will fail. If judges cooperate in and endorse the council's work, and accept the legitimacy of the resulting guidelines, the overall venture may succeed. The trick is to figure out how to involve judges in the drafting of guidelines while not letting them dominate the process.

Halliday's report set out four models for a sentencing council: Option A (the Court of Appeal sitting in a special capacity); Option B (an independent body with strong judicial leadership, appointed by the Lord Chancellor, and composed solely of judges and magistrates); Option C (an independent body with strong judicial leadership, appointed by the Lord Chancellor, and composed of judges 'as well as professionals and academics'); and Option D (an independent body appointed by the Lord Chancellor, but without reserving its leadership to the judiciary, 'and having a more even set of members') (Home Office 2001b: 55–6).

The government in the Criminal Justice Bill chose Option B. That was just about the worst possible choice. In the Criminal Justice Act, the government eventually chose a very weak form of Option C (though without academics) in which judges have a two-thirds majority of membership and the senior judiciary has a role in selecting the non-judicial minority. Judicial ownership of the council is made clear in the Act. The Lord Chief Justice is the chairman and, though any member, including a non-judicial member, may be designated as deputy chairman, only a 'person eligible for appointment as a judicial officer' may substitute for the Lord Chief Justice on occasions when he or she is absent (Section 167 [8]). In other words, a non-judicial member may be given the title of deputy chairman, but not the function of acting for the chairman in the latter's absence. The non-judicial members may sit round the table but they are not to be allowed a leadership role.

Halliday's preference for Option B was based on the belief that cooperation and support from English judges is essential, and that they will not cooperate if they are not in charge. No doubt there is some validity to this. English senior judges are influential, politically powerful and jealous of their prerogatives. US experience, however, instructs that councils composed solely of judges or dominated by them are unlikely to devise guidelines of sufficient rigour and specificity to get Halliday's jobs done.

It would have been better from a strategic policy perspective to have tried seriously to develop a meaningful set of guidelines and fail than to have adopted a half-hearted approach that cannot possibly succeed. A sentencing council run and dominated by judges will not adopt guidelines of sufficient ambition to effect major changes in sentencing practice. A council in which judges play important roles, and in which judicial members support the policies adopted, is capable of adopting ambitious policies and winning judicial support for them. So, at least, the US experience suggests.

Creation and operation of a successful sentencing council (the US term is commission, but for consistency I use 'council' here except in reference to a specific body) is not easy under the best of circumstances, including when they are not dominated by judges. More than half of the sentencing councils in the United States failed to develop and promulgate meaningful guidelines.

Some failures were absolute. Councils in Maine, Connecticut and New Mexico, for example, at the urging of their judicial members, decided that their mission was a fruitless one and produced reports opposing adoption of guidelines (von Hirsch *et al.* 1986).

Other councils, such as in New York (Griset 1991), South Carolina, and in the first instance Pennsylvania (Martin 1984), developed guidelines proposals that were rejected by legislatures. Still others, notably in Wisconsin, Tennessee, Louisiana and Florida, developed guidelines that were implemented but within a few years the legislature abolished the commission, the guidelines, or both (Tonry 1991; Reitz 2001a).

Still other councils that survived in literal terms are seen by many as substantive failures. At one extreme, Pennsylvania's council adopted presumptive guidelines that were approved (technically, not disapproved) by the legislature but were eviscerated by appellate courts that construed appellate review standards so deferentially to trial judges' discretion that the 'presumptive' guidelines are effectively voluntary (Reitz 2001a). At the other extreme, the US Sentencing Commission promulgated guidelines of such complexity and severity that they are generally characterized as a good idea gone bad (e.g. Doob 1995; Stith and Cabranes 1998).

Before discussing key issues that make councils more and less likely to succeed, it may be helpful to recall US Federal District Court Judge Marvin Frankel's original proposal. The subtitle of his book *Criminal Sentences – Law without Order* (1973) derived from his perception that sentencing in US federal courts was 'lawless,' by which he meant that sentencing judges lacked meaningful guidance by legal rules or presumptions when making decisions about offenders' liberty. He contrasted this unfavourably with tort and contract law for which legal doctrine provided such standards both for determining liability and for calculating damages.

Frankel's critique of US federal courts in 1973 applies with full force to English courts in 2004. In English courts, highly refined criminal law doctrines govern the question whether to convict, but for most cases judges have nearly unfettered discretion over sentencing.

Judge Frankel's proposed solution was the promulgation of presumptive sentencing guidelines by a specialized administrative agency. The guidelines were called 'presumptive' rather than 'voluntary' or 'mandatory' because they were meant both to preserve discretion to adjust sentences to unusual circumstances and to create strong presumptions about appropriate sentences for ordinary cases. Judges would ordinarily be expected to sentence in accordance with the guidelines, but would have authority to 'depart from the guidelines', to impose other sentences, if they provided detailed written reasons for doing so. The defendant or the state, however, could test the adequacy of the judge's reasons by appealing the 'departure' to a higher court. In voluntary guidelines, by contrast, such as England's current guidelines for magistrates, compliance by judges would be wholly voluntary, and under mandatory guidelines judges would lack discretion to depart.

Judge Frankel's proposal that the guidelines be developed by a special-purpose administrative agency was based on several arguments. One was that comprehensive sentencing policies would best be developed by a specialized body that could accumulate expertise and an institutional memory. Legislatures were seen as less able to do this job because attention spans are short and staff turnover is high. A second was that acknowledgment of the importance of democratic accountability could be achieved either actively by requiring legislative approval of proposed guidelines or passively by providing that proposed guidelines be presented to the legislature and take effect after a designated period unless rejected. A third was that a specialized agency with members appointed for fixed terms would be somewhat more insulated than are legislatures from short-term passions and concerns for political expediency. A fourth was that people might be appointed as commissioners who had specialized expertise and who represented a cross-section of interested agencies and disciplines. A fifth was that permanent staff under stable leadership could perform important collateral functions including data collection, monitoring, training, development of proposed amendments and projection of likely effects of proposed policy changes.

All of these aims have been realized by the handful of successful councils in Minnesota, Washington, Kansas, Oregon and North Carolina, and many of them have been achieved by Delaware's hybrid Sentencing Accountability Commission (Tonry 1996: chaps. 2 and 3; Reitz 2001a,b). In most of these states, councils are regularly called upon to develop impact projections of proposed statutory changes. The resulting projections are taken seriously, staff are regarded as credible, and analyses often result in refinement or abandonment of proposed statutory amendments (Boerner and Lieb 2001; Wright 2002; Frase 2004).

Councils don't, can't and shouldn't provide complete insulation from populist and other political pressures. They have, however, provided buffers that have kept policies steadier and have spared states like Minnesota, Washington, North Carolina and Delaware some of the more extreme forms of contemporary American three-strikes, truth-in-sentencing and mandatory minimum sentence laws. Minnesota and North Carolina also managed to constrain prison population growth at levels well below the national average.

That short overview is meant to demonstrate that councils can, but often do not, achieve the goals that Judge Frankel had in mind, and that the Halliday report appears to envisage. It's not easy though. The following propositions summarize what has been learned from US experience. Elsewhere I develop them at greater length (Tonry 2002).

Judicial involvement

Avoid judicial dominance. Most councils dominated by judges have failed to develop successful guidelines systems. Some of the systems developed by judges, most famously in Maryland and Florida, were defensive efforts to forestall other sentencing changes that might more fundamentally constrain judicial discretion (Carrow 1984). Many of the systems designed by judges have resulted in 'voluntary' guidelines. The evaluation literature in the US has not documented a single instance where voluntary guidelines have successfully changed sentencing patterns in a jurisdiction (Tonry 1996 chap. 2; Reitz 2001a).

This is in effect the political strategy adopted by the English judiciary. Having failed to stop the momentum of Halliday's guidelines proposals altogether, they managed to persuade the government to allow them to control the sentencing council. This is a bit like putting foxes in charge of henhouses.

Why is the record of judicial involvement so dismal? Maybe because judges by training and ideology are especially committed to the desirability of judicial discretion and reluctant to establish sentencing rules that seriously constrain that discretion. Or maybe because judges and most practising lawyers are used to focusing on one case at a time, they are less accustomed to thinking in broad policy terms than are legislators, executive branch officials and policy analysts. Whatever the reason, sentencing policy is too important a subject to be left (solely) to the judges.

One argument for judicial domination of development of sentencing guidelines warrants special mention and unequivocal refutation. This is the notion that development of sentencing standards by anyone but judges is somehow an unconstitutional violation of judicial independence. In 25 years' working on sentencing policy issues in the US, I never heard an American judge make that argument. No one there questions the authority of legislatures to define the elements of crimes, set mandatory, minimum or maximum penalties, specify sentencing criteria and create rebuttable and irrebuttable presumptions about appropriate dispositions.

In any case, in England as in America, there is no doubt that legislators have constitutional authority to enact sentencing laws of general application (Ashworth 2000: 44–8). As Lord Bingham (1996: 25) wrote concerning statute-mandated minimum sentences:

> There is room for rational argument whether it is desirable to restrict the judges' sentencing discretion in the way described or not. As parliament can prescribe a maximum penalty without infringing the constitutional independence of the judges, so it can prescribe a minimum. This is, in the widest sense, a political question – a question of what is beneficial for the polity – not a constitutional question.

Lord Bingham disposed of the constitutional point, but the beliefs, seemingly widely held among English judges, that they have unique insight into sentencing, and constitutional authority over sentencing policy, will die hard. A sentencing council led or dominated by judges holding such views is not likely to accomplish much of value.

Membership

Only a minority or bare majority of members should be judges. The council should be able to make decisions by majority vote (though ideally unanimously after vigorous debate and compromise) of members who include a majority or large minority of non-judges. Interests and values in addition to those held dear by judges are relevant. If decision processes do not give influential voice to proponents of those other issues and values, they are likely to be ignored or undervalued. There need to be enough non-judicial members to assure that deliberations and decisions take serious account of non-judicial views.

There is another practical reason why a predominantly judicial council is a bad idea. While membership need not be a full-time job, it will require frequent meetings and substantial investments of time. The members of a council consisting mostly of full-time judges and magistrates, however, are unlikely to be able to devote substantial time or energy to its work and to meet more than once a month or once a quarter.

The job is much too large for that. Drafting comprehensive guidelines is an enormous, complicated and time-consuming job and a majority of councils elsewhere have failed. Giving the job to a part-time council composed mostly of judges reduces the odds of success to near zero.

There are other reasons why many or most members should be non-judges. First, other professionals, including prosecutors, probation officers, prison officials, defence lawyers and academics possess relevant specialized knowledge. Many would argue that the views of ex-offenders, victims and treatment providers should be represented. Second, guidelines must be sold not only to judges but also to prosecutors, defence lawyers and probation officials. Each in significant ways can influence case dispositions before or after trial, or both. In the United States, members of councils, including judges, were often seen and used as points of contact with and ambassadors to their respective constituencies. A well-regarded prosecutor or probation officer may be much better placed to sell a council's proposals to his or her colleagues than can a council composed mostly of judges.

Here too the provisions of the Criminal Justice Act 2003 are misconceived. Four non-judicial members on a twelve-member council is too few. Moreover, the idea that the Home Secretary should consult the Lord Chancellor and the Lord Chief Justice before making appointments accepts rather than repudiates the notion that judges should have special influence over the council. A serious effort to develop guidelines will raise difficult issues over which there should be vigorous and unrestrained arguments. The non-judicial members should be selected on the basis that they are likely to be strong-minded and assertive proponents of their own points of view and of the institutional interests of the agencies in which they operate.

The US experience demonstrates that guidelines-setting is an inevitably political exercise that implicates both normative and institutional conflicts and that these are best dealt with openly. Creating a council consisting mostly of judicial members and of other members who have been vetted by the judicial members is unlikely to operate in this way. It would be far better to have had a majority of non-judicial members, at least some of whom were not, in the judicial view, sufficiently deferential to judicial sensibilities.

Leadership

The chair probably should be a judge, though this is not essential. Some of the most successful councils have been chaired by judges. All have included influential judges among their members. All have been independent agencies, usually in the executive branch of government.

Most of the judges who have played key roles in developing successful guidelines systems were trial judges at the time (though many were subsequently promoted to higher judicial posts).

Judges, of course, are central figures in sentencing and sentencing politics. They are the professional group whose acceptance of a new guidelines scheme will be most important to its success, and the council's credibility in the eyes of judges is therefore vital. From this perspective, having Lord Woolf chair the council, and having it known informally as the 'Woolf council', are likely to be symbolically important and reassuring to judges.

Considerably more important, though, is that the chair be a politically powerful figure committed to the guidelines and prepared to expend personal political capital to assure their adoption and implementation. Probably in England a judge is best situated to play this role if he (or, in England, most improbably, she) is committed to the goal of developing meaningful, comprehensive guidelines. If the chair is not committed to that aim, the effort will go nowhere.

In the US, where judges are less politically powerful than in England, the chairs of successful councils were often but not always judges. In Minnesota, the American jurisdiction generally said to have had the most successful council and guidelines, the key figure (though not the chair) was Judge Douglas Amdahl, at the outset a trial judge and eventually chief justice of the Minnesota Supreme Court. The Minnesota situation was in some ways the closest to English potentiality. Amdahl was an influential member of the initial council, used his personal influence and charisma to win general judicial acquiescence to the idea of guidelines, and later as chief justice of the Minnesota Supreme Court was a critical figure in developing a body of supportive appellate case law.

Judges were important in the work of other successful US councils. In North Carolina, the chair and key figure was Judge Thomas Ross, at the outset a trial judge and later director of the Administrative Office of the North Carolina Courts. In Delaware, the key figure and sometime chair was Judge Richard Gebelein; he had also previously been state Attorney General. In Washington, the key figure was Norman Maleng, the elected County Attorney of King County (Seattle). In Oregon, the key figure (though again not the chair) was the elected Oregon Attorney General Hardy Myers. Each of these people was a strong, politically savvy operator who was committed to the guidelines effort, and willing to expend personal political capital to make the effort succeed.

The Criminal Justice Act 2003 may have got this right, but by chance. Having the council chaired by whoever happens to be Lord Chief

Justice provides no assurances of commitment to a broad conception of the guidelines enterprise. As the earlier quote in this chapter from Lord Taylor makes clear, were he Lord Chief Justice now, the guidelines would appear stillborn. Among the senior English judiciary in 2004, Lord Woolf is among a handful who might take the enterprise seriously.

The role of Parliament

The guidelines should be presented to Parliament and automatically take effect a fixed number of months after the presentation date unless rejected in full by vote of Parliament. Parliament should amend the Criminal Justice Act 2003 to require that proposed guidelines be placed before it, for review and possible rejection. Parliament cannot, of course, bind itself or subsequent parliaments but the principle should be established that guidelines should be rejected in full or not at all. The rationales for a council include its development of specialized expertise and its capacity to develop a coherent set of interlocking guidelines. Piecemeal review and acceptance or rejection would be inconsistent with the notion that the council's special expertise should be respected and deferred to, and would inevitably result in anomalies when some particular provisions were rejected and others, premised on them, were not.

Requiring parliamentary acceptance (through inaction) or rejection (by vote) would place pressure on the council to develop defensible guidelines as the entire fruits of the effort could be defeated if a single controversial provision imperilled promulgation of the guidelines as a whole. The guidelines should be promulgated through inaction rather than after an affirmative vote because that gives presumptive weight to the council's decisions and makes it more likely they will be approved.

Why Parliament rather than the Court of Appeal, or the Lord Chancellor? First, the judiciary is neither the only constituency nor the only bureaucracy that has an interest in sentencing policy. Giving the judiciary the final word is in effect to provide for adoption of guidelines only to the extent and in the form the judiciary approves. Second, the council might decide on policy grounds that judicial discretion should be constrained more than judges favour. The judiciary could, of course, like any other constituency make its views known to Parliament during the review period.

The English judiciary, however, played its 'unconstitutional intrusion on judicial independence' card and persuaded the government to allow the judicially controlled council to make the final decisions about guidelines. The constitutional argument is no less a nonsense in this context than it is, as Lord Bingham noted, in the mandatory minimum sentence context. Parliament unarguably possesses constitutional authority to enact laws and general policies governing the sentencing authority of judges.

The Criminal Justice Act 2003 requires the council to 'consider whether' to frame sentencing guidelines if either the Home Secretary or the Sentencing Advisory Panel proposes it do so (Section 170 [3]). When the council 'decides to frame or revise' guidelines, it must inform the Sentencing Advisory Panel (Section 171 [1]), and when it develops draft guidelines it must publish them and consult the Home Secretary, anyone the Lord Chancellor designates, and anyone else the council chooses. The decisions, however, are entirely the council's to make.

Here too, the Criminal Justice Act 2003 got a critical point wrong. Letting the judiciary control the council, and not keeping it honest by the implied threat that guidelines too deferential to judicial sensibilities would be rejected by the Parliament, is unlikely to result in development of meaningful guidelines.

Appointment of members

A majority of a sentencing council's members should be appointed by the executive branch. The key point is that all or most should not be appointed by the judiciary. There are a number of alternate approaches. Enabling legislation can identify categories of members (judges, prosecutors, corrections officials, legislators, victim advocates, etc.) and empower the executive branch (in England, the Home Secretary) to appoint them. Or various branches of government can be given appointment authority: the judiciary over judges, the legislative branch over legislators, the executive branch over all others. Or agencies could be given appointment power: the heads of the Crown Prosecution Service, the Probation Service, the Prison Service, the Association of Chief Police Officers, for example, could be empowered to designate members from their professional communities.

Dispersed appointment powers make sense on a number of grounds. For formal and substantive reasons, the Lord Chancellor is in an especially good position to select judicial members. There is, however, no reason to impute comparative advantage to the Lord Chancellor concerning appointment of prosecutors, probation and prison officials, academics or other non-judicial members. The Home Secretary through the Home Office staff interacts professionally and regularly with these groups and has much more extensive experience and networking on which to draw. And heads of professional groups have even more knowledge of people working within their professions.

Hybrid appointment schemes are common in the US. All appointments to the seven-member US Sentencing Commission were made by the US President with the advice and consent of the US Senate. Three of the seven members, however, had to be judges selected from a longer list of nominees put forward by the Chief Justice of the US Supreme Court. Elsewhere, details varied from state to state but the most typical model called for the state governor to make some appointments, the state legislature to make some and the state supreme court to make some.

The Criminal Justice Act adopts about the worst of all possible approaches. I've already explained why having a majority judicial membership is a mistake. Giving the Lord Chancellor unrestricted authority to appoint the judicial members creates large risks that the council will be dominated by members who are hostile to the very idea of ambitious guidelines. Requiring the Home Secretary to consult the senior judiciary about possible non-judicial appointees gives the judiciary influence even over those choices. It is difficult to imagine a Home Secretary appointing someone known to be uncongenial to the judiciary. The appointment system chosen is wrong on the merits. It's also wrong in its symbolism, for it appears to acknowledge judicial ownership of sentencing policy.

In the end, the success of a guidelines system depends on the technical knowledge, policy sophistication, political acumen and leadership of the body that creates it. More councils have gone wrong than right, and no set of structural arrangements can assure success. However, experience suggests choices among structural alternatives that can make success more and less likely. Strong, committed leadership and a well-chosen membership are essential to the success of a sentencing council. Get these seriously wrong, and the venture is highly unlikely to succeed.

What a serious guidelines development process would entail

In the introduction to this chapter I set out a conspiracy theory for development of ambitious guidelines by stealth. It depended on there being an understanding among Lord Woolf, the Home Secretary and others that comprehensive guidelines are the true aim; that the Sentencing Advisory Panel or the Home Secretary will effectively propose development of comprehensive guidelines; that Lord Woolf in leading the council's 'consideration' of those proposals will achieve a decision to do so; and that Lord Woolf will then lead both the development effort and the equally important effort to persuade the judiciary to acquiesce in good faith in their implementation.

As a person who seldom gets closer to the corridors of power than to change trains in the Westminster tube station, I've no particular reason to believe such an understanding exists. If it does, it is unlikely to succeed. On the off chance, however, that such aspirations are real, this section discusses some of the major actions the council would have to take to develop meaningful comprehensive guidelines of the sort Halliday proposed.

A sentencing council's key functions are the development and successful implementation of presumptive sentencing guidelines for all offences. The English sentencing council will need experienced administrative and research staff and sufficient money to complete a serious guidelines development process, should the council, somewhat improbably, attempt one. Because the Act merely empowers, rather than requires, the council to develop guidelines, and not necessarily or even probably comprehensive ones, the work does not necessarily entail any particular process.

This section somewhat counterfactually assumes that the council will choose to develop comprehensive guidelines of the sort Halliday envisioned, and comments on how that might best be done. The process perforce would include widespread consultation concerning particular subjects and successive iterations of draft guidelines; a combination of original data collection and analysis of existing data sets to provide baseline data for policy purposes, for forecasting and for evaluation of guidelines operation and effects; and development of capacities for training judges and other practitioners at the outset and providing ongoing training and technical assistance after implementation.

In the medium and long terms, the council will need resources for ongoing monitoring and training, evaluation, and ongoing refinement of the guidelines. Both to inform policy-making and take advantage of the uniquely rich data sets commissions typically create, ongoing work should include an active programme of intramural and extramural research.

A governing rationale

The council needs to agree on a governing rationale or purpose. Sentencing guidelines succeed when and because they make normative and policy sense. More overtly in the US but inevitably also in England, judicial and other practitioners choose whether and how to comply with statutes, rules and guidelines. From here on in this chapter, I use the word 'rules' to mean all of these. Rules that practitioners consider unwise, unfeasible or unjust are seldom enforced with vigour or integrity. This is why mandatory minimum sentencing laws are inconsistently and often unjustly applied. Conversely, if practitioners understand the logic and underlying principles of a rule, they are more likely to apply it consistently and fairly even if they disagree with it. This is the American experience with successful guidelines systems. A council's first order of business consequently should be to work on and provisionally adopt a saleable rationale and set of purposes.

Setting general purposes of sentencing is easy. Few people disagree that primary purposes include crime prevention and reduction, affirmation of widely held moral values and imposition of deserved punishments. Others might add something about victims. Reasonable people can quickly reach agreement about purposes when stated at this level of abstraction.

Neither the White Paper, the Criminal Justice Bill nor the Criminal Justice Act gives much guidance on purposes. All set out laundry lists. The White Paper sets out these purposes: protect the public, punish, reduce crime, deter, incapacitate, reform and rehabilitate, and promote reparation (Home Office 2002a: 87–8). Section 142 of the Criminal Justice Act 2003 says about the same thing: punish offenders, reduce crime (including through deterrence, reform, and rehabilitation), protect the public and promote reparation. Halliday, more economically, referred to crime reduction, reparation and punishment, and more coherently proposed an explicit limiting retributivist penal philosophy.

The problem with all those lists is that the various possible purposes often conflict in individual cases, and the lists give no guidance at all as to how they are to be reconciled. A person convicted of a comparatively minor offence such as shoplifting or sale of marijuana, for example, might be seen to present significant risks for future violence. Should notions of deserved punishment be paramount, and limit the sentence to what may be justly imposed for shoplifting; or should crime-reduction concerns be made paramount, in which case a much longer sentence might be ordered?

Neither the White Paper nor the Criminal Justice Bill or Act provides an answer. The Criminal Justice Act 1991 tried: the punishment should be commensurate with the seriousness of the offence. Halliday also tried. Except for a small and carefully defined category of dangerous offenders, his limiting retributivist ideas would limit punishments to the maximum that the seriousness of the offence (and relevant and recent prior convictions) would justify. Beyond that, crime-reduction goals would be trumped by considerations of justice.

Since the Criminal Justice Act 2003 does not provide a rationale for punishment that will explicitly or implicitly set priorities among punishment's possible purposes, the sentencing council will have to do it. This will not be easy. Reasonable people have divergent but powerful intuitions about just punishment. The people who drew up the 1991 Act, and the scholars on whose work they drew and relied, meant for the 1991 Act to be premised on desert rationales and accordingly meant and understood the term 'commensurate' when applied to punishment to mean 'commensurate [or proportionate] with the gravity of the offence'. This presumably seemed straightforward or obvious to them. To the judges who decided *Cunningham*, which gutted the desert rationale in favour of 'punishment and deterrence', it must have seemed equally straightforward and obvious that judges must take account of what they see as an inexorable need for deterrence.

I drew the preceding paragraph's contrast a bit tendentiously, but for emphasis. The point is that, whatever the deterrence literature may show, and despite Halliday's conclusion that there is no 'evidence to support making deterrence a specific purpose of sentencing in individual cases' (Home Office 2001b: 9), many judges believe themselves to be in the marginal deterrence business. Ignoring this, the 1991 Act experience shows, leads to foreseeable judicial resistance. Recognizing this last, however, emphasizes the importance of persuading judges that policies are sound, legitimate and principled. If the council itself cannot reach and then justify choices in such matters, the guidelines will be incoherent or unpersuasive. Neither adjective gives grounds for confidence that sentencing judges will enthusiastically accept and apply guidelines.

US experience indicates that people of good will working together can reach and then explain decisions about rationales, and accordingly can explain and justify decisions based on those rationales. This is a major part of the Washington, Oregon and North Carolina guidelines stories, in which judges were initially reluctant participants but eventually became active proponents and helped convince the judiciary at large that guidelines were sound in principle and wise in policy. Most US councils adopted some form of desert or limiting retributivism as their governing rationale. The US federal commission refused to adopt a rationale and many observers attribute the federal guidelines' incoherence, excessive severity and lack of credibility to this decision and its consequences (Stith and Cabranes 1998).

The Halliday report opted for limiting retributivism, but of a vague sort. In the abstract, most versions of limiting retributivism offer three major claims. Offenders cannot justly be punished more severely than their current offence deserves. Offenders should never be punished more severely than the minimum they deserve unless there are good articulated reasons for doing so. Within those bounds, other considerations may justify the imposition of different sentences on offenders convicted of comparable crimes.

Whatever decision the council initially makes, however, should be provisional. Consideration of particular issues (for example, taking account of prior offences or sentencing for concurrent offences) may indicate that no policy response that commands wide support is consistent with the initial rationale. Sometimes the solution will be to defer a decision and think about it some more. Sometimes the solution will be to revisit a provisional rationale that, the council may decide, needs refinement or qualification.

Comprehensiveness

The guidelines adopted should be comprehensive and cover at least all offences for which imprisonment may be ordered. The Home Office seems to understand this (Blunkett 2004), even if the Act does not provide for it. The key point is that guidelines should include all regularly recurring offences for which prison can be imposed, including burglary, theft, receiving stolen goods, garden variety assaults, minor drug crimes and driving while intoxicated or while under suspension. Wide breadth of coverage is substantively important.

The Halliday proposals if adopted would effect a major change in sentencing policies and practices and the guidelines' main aim is to facilitate their implementation. Equally importantly, wide coverage forces policy-makers to consider options in light of other choices. If, for example, stranger rape is punishable with a four-year prison sentence, can a four-year sentence be justified for a fifth-time low-value, commercial burglar? Or, if a decision is made to increase the starting point for stranger rape sentences from four to eight years, for what other offences should sentences be reduced, and by how much, to implement the rape sentencing decisions within existing resources? Development of comprehensive guidelines forces attention to such questions.

Ranking of offences

The council should develop its own ranking of offence severity. This obscure but important point raises fundamental questions of constitutional and political theory for some people. The problem is that comprehensive guidelines require classification of offences into a manageable number of categories on the basis of their seriousness. Almost all people, regardless of the punishment theory or rationale they espouse, share powerful intuitions about proportionality: more serious crimes deserve severer penalties than less serious crimes (the 'proportionality principle') and comparably serious crimes deserve comparably severe penalties (the 'equality principle'). In order to devise comprehensive guidelines, some method must be used to identify comparably serious offences that can be put into particular offence seriousness categories.

The difficulty is that in no common-law jurisdiction, including England and Wales, does legislation provide sufficient guidance for the necessary sorting. In most countries' criminal laws, maximum sentences are inconsistent. As a result, grouping crimes in accordance with maximum sentences authorized by statute will not provide a coherent or normatively justifiable classification system. Maxima for particular offences are the products of transient passions caused by notorious crimes or of the idiosyncratic beliefs of ministers who happened to be in office when particular laws were passed. Considered in isolation, authorized penalties for particular offences may make sense. Seen as a whole, considering all offences, maximum authorized penalties are riddled with anomalies.

Most American sentencing councils devised their own systems of offence classification, largely because the legislative classes were over-broad and insufficiently discriminating. In many states, offences were described generically and councils decided that various sub-categories of offence warranted different seriousness rankings. For example, robbery permutations with and without guns, with and without victim injury, with and without high property loss might all fall into different offence seriousness categories. Some legislative classifications were simply seen as unsound, the products of a passing moral panic or political expediency. These decisions were not controversial or seen (by most people) to raise constitutional issues, because US guidelines are invariably put before the legislature for active or passive consideration.

In England, this issue may be more controversial than in the US Offences are not classified in English law except implicitly by reference to maximum authorized sentences, and very broadly in terms of whether indictable, summary or triable either way. From this it might be inferred that Parliament has classified all offences (all subject to maximum sentence x or x plus or minus y per cent are deemed in one class, etc.). Almost undoubtedly, such an inferred classification system will be incoherent and full of anomalies. This is not surprising since criminal penalty legislation tends to be adopted piecemeal, and seldom to be reconsidered, so over time the whole is a product of a wide range of different times, personalities and cultural norms about punishment.

The council should largely ignore any implied parliamentary classification logic and devise its own. If the guidelines are facially incoherent or arbitrary, and classify together offences that in day-to-day understanding are of substantially different seriousness, they will lack credibility altogether. They will necessarily prescribe comparably severe sentences for offences that are generally seen as substantially different in their seriousness. This violates the equality principle.

The answer for England is that the council must classify offence seriousness in its own way. This has in practice seldom proved difficult elsewhere. Research in many countries and US sentencing council experience show that Western peoples, at least, have widely shared beliefs about offence seriousness.

Should constitutional concern for deference to implied parliamentary classifications be seen as a serious problem, the enabling legislation should be amended to require that the proposed guidelines be placed before Parliament for passive or active consideration (but subject to a proviso that the guidelines must be accepted or rejected in their entirety).

Drafting guidelines afresh

The council must draft guidelines *de novo*, comprehensively and from the ground up rather than attempt to augment the existing body of guideline judgements. The White Paper and the Bill appear at times to contemplate, and the Act accepts, that guidelines be developed piecemeal, by engrafting successive changes and expansions onto the existing body of guideline judgements announced by the Court of Appeal.

Unfortunately, it doesn't and can't possibly work that way. Comprehensive guidelines cannot be drafted from the top down, taking existing guidelines and building around them. One reason this doesn't work is that gross anomalies inevitably will arise. It will be sheer coincidence, for example, if guidelines for burglary involving a theft and possession of a gun called for the same sentence as guidelines for robbery involving the same amount of property, the same location, and possession of a gun.

Another, much more important reason it can't work is that drafting comprehensive guidelines necessarily entails policy trade-offs. If longer sentences for sex crimes are wanted, then sentences for something else must be shortened. Looking at the sentencing system, and sentences, as a whole is an inherent part of drafting comprehensive guidelines. It can't be done piecemeal.

The process of drafting guidelines will have to begin by commissioning research into past sentencing practices. This will be necessary for use in modelling the likely effects of alternative guidelines under consideration and will be needed later on for evaluating compliance with guidelines and measuring their effects. Existing Home Office data and routinely compiled official statistics are unlikely to be adequate for these purposes, for two reasons. First, data must be collected on offence and offender characteristics for individual offenders as they were processed through the system. Existing data systems report aggregate rather than offender-based or transactional data.

Second, data will be necessary that are not now routinely collected. These will include such things as the original charges, any charges dismissed, whether the defendant pleaded guilty and at what point, the offence of conviction, and the sentence imposed. Rich information will also be needed on individual offenders' prior criminal records, on the circumstances of the current offence (violence, weapons, co-offenders, property loss), and on offenders' personal characteristics (age, gender, ethnicity, employment record and skills, family responsibilities). Data on past practices and sentences will be needed on every subject that might be incorporated into the guidelines.

These data can then be used to identify current sentencing practices for particular crimes and particular kinds of offenders. Policy decisions will then need to be made whether to base guidelines on current practice. These data will also need to be used in projecting the effects of guidelines being considered. It is not possible that guidelines so developed will magically fit within the resources and personnel available to deal with them. Choices will have to be made and the baseline data will be essential for use in projections of the effects of alternative policies under consideration. None of this could be done if the existing guideline judgements were regarded as blocks of granite to be worked around. The existing guideline judgements of the Court of Appeal will have to go.

Projections of impact

The council should be required to carry out and publish impact projections for its final proposed set of guidelines. Provision of state resources to operate corrections systems should reflect policy decisions about levels and priorities of public expenditure. The council should establish a policy that the guidelines it develops will, when implemented, in light of stated and reasonable assumptions about case flows and compliance patterns, be consonant with existing and planned probation and prison system capacities (both physical and human).

David Blunkett has endorsed this view, though perhaps without understanding its prison–use–limiting implications, '[T]he Sentencing Guidelines Council needs to provide guidance that takes account of the capacity of prison and probation' (Blunkett 2004: 13).

This proposal is simple good government. There are no free lunches. Public investments should be the product of deliberate public policy choices. A resource constraint policy forces realism on policy makers: if severer penalties are wanted for offence x, there must either be facilities available to deliver those penalties or decisions must be made to reduce penalties for other offences or to increase public investment.

Aggregate sentences

The council should adopt a policy that no number of offences in the same seriousness category can be sentenced in aggregate to a sentence more severe than the most severe sentence authorized in guidelines for the most serious offence in that category. This concerns the question how to set a just sentence when several offences are being considered simultaneously. England has got this right, under the label of the 'totality principle' and the US has got it wrong. The emphasized proposal might be thought of as the strong version of the totality principle. A weaker version would limit penalties for offences of the same type to the most severe that could be imposed for an offence in the next higher offence severity category.

The Halliday report would preserve the totality principle, described as follows: '[W]hen several offences are sentenced together, the combined effect should be more severe than would have been justified by the most serious offence, but not so severe as to be outside the range for that offence' (Home Office 2001b: 13). If a defendant were being sentenced for 20 household burglaries, or for one burglary and 19 shopliftings, the aggregate sentence could not exceed that which would otherwise be justified for a serious burglary. Or another example, if the range of appropriate sentences for shoplifting is 0–12 months and for burglary 12–24 months, for 20 shoplifting incidents a strong version of the totality principle would limit the aggregate sentence to 12 months and a weak version to 24 months. The leading common-law analysts who have considered the problem have endorsed the totality principle (Lovegrove 1989; Ashworth 2000: 226-30) and Swedish (Jareborg 1998) and Dutch (Tak 2001) practice embody it.

I may be belabouring the point a bit since Halliday proposed retaining the totality principle. I do so because a logic that every prior offence warrants an increment of additional punishment for each successive offence, often associated with Jack Straw when Home Secretary, is expressly endorsed in the White Paper, the Bill and the Act. This is not exactly the same subject but is parallel ('Each current offence warrants an additional increment of punishment') and raises similar issues of principle. It would be a pity if an English sentencing council failed to preserve so widely admired a feature of existing practice.

Prior convictions

The council should adopt a policy strictly limiting the extent to which the punishment for a current offence can be increased on account of prior convictions. This proposition is based on similar premises as the totality principle: deserved punishments should be proportionate to the culpability expressed by the primary current offence. Many people have an intuition that offenders who have previously been convicted of a crime should be dealt with more harshly, all else being equal, than offenders who have not been previously convicted. Different arguments can be offered for why that should be so – because previous convictions offer bases for stronger predictions of subsequent offending, because a person who has offended previously is somehow more culpable than a first offender, because first offenders receive a benefit-of-the-doubt discount that they lose when sentenced subsequently, or because subsequent offending is a manifestation of defiance against the state or the court. Whatever the reason, however, respect for proportionality concerns should dictate that the primary determinant of a just sentence be the offence for which it is imposed. The Halliday report's recommendation that sentences be based on the current offence and 'recent and relevant prior' convictions is defensible on principle only if qualified in a way such as I have proposed.

England having got the right idea with the totality principle, a sentencing council might well be able to get a parallel principle right for addressing the relevance of prior 'recent and relevant' convictions.

A sentencing council must address many subjects besides these, including how guilty pleas should be handled, the form guidelines will take (including grids and narrative statements), and whether 'discounts' will be available for younger offenders. Those set out above are among the most important.

*　　*　　*　　*

Judges are part of the sentencing policy problem and must be part of the solution. They are part of the problem by definition. They make many of the crucial decisions in individual cases. For any change in sentencing policy to work, judges will have to change the way they do business and accept restraints on their discretion.

They are also part of the problem ideologically in England and in most countries. Judges tend to believe that sentencing is a craft that cannot except very crudely be subjected to rules, that judges have special understanding of sentencing, and accordingly that the best sentencing systems will be those that give large discretions to judges. Judges' centrality in the process and their common belief in their need for discretion mean that they often are fierce and effective opponents of proposed changes in sentencing policy or practice. If the weight of judicial opinion is strongly opposed to a sentencing policy innovation, they will try to kill it, as they killed the Criminal Justice Act 1991 and as they tried to prevent the enactment of mandatory minimum sentences in the late 1990s. They may through public opposition prevent adoption of changes in sentencing laws or policies, as they tried to do in relation to a sentencing council and guidelines. They did not stop parliamentary enactment of the council and guidelines provisions of the Criminal Justice Act 2003, but they succeeded in obtaining statutory language highly deferential to the judiciary and highly unlikely to result in promulgation of meaningful guidelines.

Judges must therefore be part of the solution. No guidelines system can succeed unless prevailing judicial sentiment is kindly disposed. In modern jargon, this is an issue of legitimacy. If judges do not see guidelines as principled and sensible and a reasonable accommodation of competing values and goals, they will be seen as an illegitimate intrusion on judicial discretion and as a source of unjust outcomes.

How can judges be won over? First, the council must be seen by judges to be credible. The government went too far in giving judges the chairmanship and too large a fraction of the positions on the council, and in various ways giving the senior judiciary too much influence over the process. Recoupment will require that Lord Woolf be committed to the guidelines enterprise and willing to devote his energies and authority to persuading the judiciary of the need for meaningful change.

Second, the council must always be concerned about practical matters of implementation, about the processes by which new policies must be carried out if they are to succeed. Partly this is a matter of credibility. If a proposed policy is likely to be seen by judges as unworkable, or raises serious foreseeable implementation problems, one way or another the council must adapt accordingly. Either the policy must be changed or a feasible solution to the implementation impediment must be put forward.

Third, very substantial thought and resources must be invested in educating the judiciary and all affected practitioners about the guidelines development process and about the guidelines ultimately adopted and the reasons why they were adopted. The goal, put differently, is to persuade judges and others that the proposed guidelines are a 'Good Thing'.

There are grounds for pessimism that the English judiciary may be so indisposed to the development of guidelines that meaningfully restrain sentencing judges' discretion that the chances of success are too low to justify the effort. Only time will tell.

Creation of a sentencing council and development and implementation of meaningful guidelines could make English sentencing more consistent, transparent and predictable; reduce the scale of racial, ethnic and gender disparities; provide a tool for management and control of state resources devoted to punishment of offenders; and make judges more accountable for their decisions about citizens' liberties.

It is more than time to bring the rule of law to English sentencing. Sentencing concerns the state's deprivation of individuals' liberty or property because they have reliably been adjudged to have violated fundamental behavioural standards. At present, though English law observes a wide variety of evidentiary, procedural and processual standards aimed at assuring justice in adjudication (though the 2003 Criminal Justice Act weakens some of these), it contains few such standards aimed at assuring justice in punishment. Most conspicuously, save for the Court of Appeal guideline judgements, whose scope is narrow and whose influence is uncertain, and statutory provisions setting maximum (and a few minimum) sentences, English law contains no rules governing the nature and amounts of punishment. Sentencing in England in 2004, like the US sentencing described by Judge Marvin Frankel in 1973, is lawless, and irrefutable evidence demonstrates gross and unjustifiable inconsistency in sentences received by like-situated offenders. A large burden has been placed on Lord Woolf's shoulders.

Chapter 6

Violence

Criminal violence in England and Wales is in decline and has been since the mid-1990s. Punishment of violent offenders became substantially harsher over that period. The parts of *Justice for All*, the White Paper, that deal with violent crimes read like and are afterthoughts, appended for the most part to political and policy worries about serious sexual crimes involving children. However, the portions of the Criminal Justice Act that deal with 'dangerous' offenders, though not without some subtlety, lack restraint and could easily result in harsh and unjustly severe punishments of offenders who aren't dangerous at all.

The most interesting question about the White Paper's violence proposals is not whether they were well developed and explained (they weren't), or whether they adequately balanced concerns for public protection and defendants' interests (they didn't), but why the government felt obliged to propose them at all. Throughout the 1990s the percentages of convicted violent and sex offenders sent to prison steadily increased, nearly doubling, and sentences became longer. From a policy perspective the most urgent challenge is to devise politically credible ways to reduce the severity of sentences for violent crimes.

Instead, introduced by polemic about a public 'sick and tired' of dangerous offenders 'who get off lightly', the White Paper offered poorly explained and immoderate proposals of a sort that might be expected if there were a public panic about violent crime. Had the Conservative Party chosen to respond demagogically, the White Paper positioned England for the kind of upward rhetorical cycle that produced three-strikes laws in more than half the American states and life sentences without possibility of pardon or parole in most.

Why might this be? Two explanations stand out. One would concentrate on reduced tolerance of risks in 'late modern society', punitive public attitudes and the cynicism of a political class that chooses to pander to public fears and primitive passions. This kind of analysis could be undertaken in any industrialized society, but only a handful of others (the US, parts of Australia) have adopted policies like those England has considered and adopted. Heightened awareness of risks and 'populist punitiveness' may have influenced policy-making in England, but they can't be the whole story, or they would have had similar effects everywhere.

The other explanation would concentrate on an emerging and distinctive set of English attitudes towards victimization and vindictiveness that risk panicked overreactions to awful events. The immediate and years-after reactions to the James Bulger, Sarah Payne and Soham cases offer examples, as in other areas do the Hatfield train crash, the Dunblane shootings and the Stephen Lawrence case.

Comparison of reactions in a number of countries to child-on-child murders provides a richer example of what may be a distinctively English problem. Two 10-year-olds killed 2-year-old James Bulger. They were held in jail for 9 months without counselling or psychological treatment, tried as adults, and sentenced to 8 years. Both Lord Taylor and Home Secretary Michael Howard felt moved successively (but ultimately unsuccessfully) to lengthen their sentences. When they were eventually released with new names, there was much media gnashing of teeth and genuine fear that their identities and whereabouts would be revealed by the press (Smith 1994; Young 1996).

In Trondheim, Norway, 5-year-old Silje Redegard was stripped, stoned, beaten and left for dead on a Friday by two 6-year-old boys. The two boys returned to school amidst a general view in the school, the community and child welfare services that the urgent need was to help the boys live through the experience with as little lasting damage as possible. Media coverage was slight, there were no vigilante crowds, the boys were neither objectified not demonized, and the victim's mother said that she believed in time she would be able to forgive the two boys (Clifford 1996; Muncie 2002).

In Chicago in 1994, 5-year-old Eric Morse was dropped from a 14th-storey window by two boys who were then 10 and 11 years old. They were angry with him because he had refused to steal sweets for them from a corner shop. Unlike in Norway, there was a firestorm of media coverage and political reaction and the Illinois legislature enacted laws providing for potentially tougher youth prisons. Unlike in England, the case was tried in a juvenile court (trial as adults was not possible). The judge throughout expressed both her sense of horror at their act and her determination that the accused children be provided adequate treatment and support services. One of the boys at 16 committed a homosexual rape in youth prison and was sentenced to a seven-year term for that crime. The other, illiterate when the crime occurred and with a long record of police stops for drug and property offences, blossomed in the services-rich youth institution where he was held, was released on licence, and graduated on schedule from the public high school in his community. The media coverage of his high-school graduation was positive.

The point of the three stories is that something in English political and popular culture conduces to sustained media and public over-reaction to horrifying events that can be blamed on someone. It is a cultural trait that policy-makers need to recognize and worry about. In that context, the White Paper's relatively slight discussion of sentencing and corrections policies for violent crimes – only several pages – can probably best be understood as symbolic or expressive. The latest celebrated cases – Sarah Payne and the children kidnapped and murdered in Soham – though indubitably violent crimes are better understood as sexual crimes against children and as such they provoke powerful visceral reactions. Overreaction to specific crimes is not a sensible foundation on which to erect general policies.

Recommendations concerning violence in the White Paper are nearly always characterized as policies for dangerous sexual and violent offenders. The focus is on sexual offences, especially against children, and the discussion of other violence is an afterthought. That being so, it is not surprising that the proposals in the White Paper and the Criminal Justice Bill were not well elaborated, well argued or well documented. The provisions enacted in the Criminal Justice Act share many of the defects of the White Paper's proposals.

Violent and sexual offences are the crimes that most worry people. Antisocial behaviour, yobs and persistent minor offenders particularly trouble the Labour government, but they are irritants, not fundamental threats to people's ability to live secure and satisfying lives. All of us know that environmental, white collar and mafia-style organized crime can cause enormous amounts of damage. So do drug abuse and trafficking. They are all troubling and important, but the threats they represent are, for most people, distant and abstract rather than concrete and immediate. As the title of a 1998 book by Zimring and Hawkins tells it, however, 'Crime is not the problem'; violence, including sexual violence, is.

This chapter examines recent policy proposals and Criminal Justice Act 2003 provisions in relation to violent crimes, for the most part artificially excluding sexual crimes from the discussion. A recent article by Matravers and Hughes (2003) examines proposals for sexual offences and offenders in considerable detail, as does a recent book by Matravers (2003).

Violence being a subject 'of critical importance to the public' (Home Office 2002a: 95), it is odd that the plethora of recent Labour government policy statements on crime and punishment said very little about violence except by rote and hyperbole. The government's 2001 pre-election policy statement, *Criminal Justice: The Way Ahead*, merely mentioned legislation enacted in 1997 and 2000, referred to forthcoming proposals concerning mentally disordered offenders, announced that the Probation Service would soon be consulting victims of violent and sexual crimes about restrictions placed on offenders leaving prison, and rightly celebrated the £206 million awarded to victims of violent crime in 1999–2000 by the Criminal Injuries Compensation Authority (Home Office 2001a: 48, 73–4). Witness intimidation was discussed for a few paragraphs, and repeat victimization of domestic violence victims was mentioned several times in passing; but nowhere is violence generally discussed as an important social problem in its own right.

The Halliday report didn't do much more (Home Office 2001b: paras. 4.5, 4.6, 4.25–4.35). In developing comprehensive proposals for overhauling sentencing and punishment policies and practices, it made only cursory references to violent crime. It proposed a 'special' type of sentence for offenders who did not fall within the ambit of legislation on mentally disordered offenders but were nonetheless 'dangerous'. Unlike all other non-life-sentence prisoners, who would be released into community supervision after serving half the announced sentence, 'dangerous' offenders could be held for the full sentence unless released by the Parole Board and, in addition, could be subjected to up to ten years extended supervision in the community thereafter. Halliday did not propose the repeal of existing laws authorizing discretionary life sentences for manslaughter, rape, robbery, wounding with intent or arson, or mandatory life sentences for second serious violent or sexual offences.

Much that is ambiguous and analytically unsatisfactory in Halliday's proposals is discussed below. The more important point is that, whatever the proposals' deficiencies for those 'dangerous' offenders who are not subject to life sentences, these provisions could not possibly apply to more than a few hundred violent crimes in any one year. Yet the *Criminal Statistics 2000* report 733,374 recorded violent and sexual crimes in 2000–01 (Home Office 2001c: table 2.15).

The recent White Paper, *Justice for All* (Home Office 2002a), is the most disappointing of these documents. *Criminal Justice: The Way Ahead* was a political document, meant to document Labour's initiatives and set out its proposals in the run-up to an election. It could be expected to accentuate the politically positive in Labour's policies and to prefer declaration over explanation. It did both. Halliday's was a report by a civil servant who no doubt felt constrained in examining subjects such as mandatory minimum sentences that Labour had just implemented and that were not part of his remit. *Justice for All*, however, purported to be a White Paper, a form of document in which one might expect to find careful policy analyses and well-reasoned arguments. Instead, amidst overheated rhetoric, the White Paper endorsed Halliday's proposals concerning violence but added various repressive measures.

The discussion of sentencing for violent and sexual offences in *Justice for All* begins with these words: 'The public are sick and tired of a sentencing system that does not make sense. They read about dangerous, violent, sexual, and other serious offenders who get off lightly, or are not in prison long enough …' (2002a: 86). The first of those two sentences is merely polemical. The second, in its allusion to reading, presumably refers to the tabloids' misleading and sensationalized coverage of notorious cases and suggests that the tabloid version of reality is the one in which the government prefers to operate.

That second sentence raises empirical issues that are not discussed (What does the public believe? Are public beliefs accurate?) or asserts as true propositions that are not demonstrated (serious offenders get off lightly or are not in prison long enough). The statement about public attitudes would be a nonsensical basis for policy development. Masses of public opinion data show that public beliefs about sentencing are misinformed. English lay people generally believe sentences are less harsh than they really are, and would themselves recommend sentences that are less severe than are now commonly imposed (Home Office 2001b: app. 5).

The lenient-sentences rhetoric is also perverse. Sentencing for violent crimes became much harsher after the early 1990s. Halliday showed that the likelihood that people convicted of indictable sexual or violent offences were sentenced to imprisonment nearly doubled between 1989 and 1999. In 1989, 18 per cent of those convicted of offences against the person were committed to custody; in 1999, 34 per cent. For sexual offences, 35 per cent received immediate custody in 1989, 66 per cent in 1999 (Home Office 2001b: app. 2, table 2).

Average prison sentence lengths also increased between 1989 and 1999, from 15.5 to 16.2 months for violent offences and from 35.4 to 37.8 months for sexual offences (app. 2, table 4). Averages, however, based on all people sentenced to prison greatly understate increases in sentence severity during a time when more people are being sent to prison. This is because the additional people will have committed less serious offences. In 1989, for example, the third of convicted sex offenders who received immediate custody were by definition the third who committed the most serious crimes. When in 1999, two-thirds received immediate custody, the extra third will have committed, on average, much less serious crimes than the first third. When the percentage of offenders receiving prison sentences goes up, average sentence lengths should go down. Thus even the seemingly modest increases in average sentences signal a substantial increase in the lengths of prison sentences.

The best way to show how sentence lengths have changed would be to compare sentences at different times for people convicted of specific narrowly defined crimes who have accumulated comparable criminal records. Off-the-shelf Home Office data do not allow this, but Table 6.1 shows an analysis that gives a crude but powerful demonstration that sentences have become much more severe. It divides prison sentences received for violent and sexual offences in 1989 and 1999 into three groups – those receiving short sentences up to six months, those receiving sentences of six months up to six years, and those receiving extremely long sentences of six years or more.

Had sentence lengths in 1999 been the same as in 1989, a very large increase in the percentages receiving short sentences could be expected, together with a decrease in the percentage receiving mid-length sentences, and a large decrease in the percentage receiving very long sentences. These things would be expected because most of the additional people sentenced to prison in 1999 would be people deemed in 1999 not to warrant any prison sentence at all, and thus in 1999 to warrant only short sentences.

What Table 6.1 shows instead are modest increases (around 20%) in the fractions receiving short sentences, modest (10–15%) decreases in the fractions receiving middling sentences, and huge increases (34–43%) in the fractions receiving very long sentences.

So claims about offenders getting off lightly deserve elaboration and justification if they are to serve as the basis for policy-making. The

Table 6.1 Changes in confinement sentence lengths, 1989 and 1999

	Up to 6 months	6 months – 6 years	6 years to life
Sexual offences			
1989	7%	76.6%	15.5%
1999	9	68.5	22.2
Absolute difference	+2	–8.1	+6.7
Percentage difference	(+28.5%)	(–15.7%)	(+43.2%)
Violent offences			
1989	28%	66.5%	4.8%
1999	34	59.8	6.5
Absolute difference	+6	–6.7	+1.7
Percentage difference	(+21.4%)	(–10.1%)	(+33.6%)

Source: Home Office 2002b: Appendix 2, table 4

problem with sentencing for violent crime is not that it is too light but that it has become too severe. This will be a formidable problem for developers of sentencing guidelines to overcome.

The proposals for violent (and sexual) offenders in the White Paper *Justice for All* are set out in five short declaratory paragraphs that neither explain nor justify them. They are, as noted, essentially Halliday's proposals, somewhat augmented. As in Halliday's report, the only violent offences receiving special attention are the few hundreds that might fall within dangerous-offender legislation. Also as in Halliday's report, the crucial criteria for application of the dangerous-offender provisions are not discussed (which offences could serve as predicates, what level of risk must be shown, what kinds of future harms count?). Halliday openly worried that his (milder) proposals were 'potentially very onerous and punitive' (Home Office 2001b: 33). *Justice for All* reveals little humility or ambivalence about the powers it would grant the state over citizens' lives.

This chapter identifies and examines issues that Halliday, the White Paper, the Bill and the Act raised and others they should have addressed. The first section, to set the stage, examines criminal violence in England since 1990. Threshold questions include whether violence is getting worse and, after that, whether there is reason to believe that current policies and practices are insufficient. Overall, the prevalence of criminal violence in England is stable or declining, though changes in reporting and recording practices obscure this. Crime trends provide no reason to believe that England is suffering a crisis in violent crime or that any extraordinary measures are needed to address it. Politicians generally claim credit for good things that happen while they are in power. In relation to violent crime, existing policies appear to have 'worked'.

The second section examines sentencing and punishment practices in relation to violence. Since 1989, sentences for violent (and sexual) crimes have become much harsher, and are a major driver of the rising prison population. The probability has doubled that an offender convicted of an indictable violent offence will be sentenced to imprisonment, and lengths of prison sentences have steadily risen. This has important implications for development of sentencing guidelines.

The third section raises a series of issues concerning sentencing and punishment of violent offenders that have been overlooked but must be addressed if sentencing guidelines are to be developed. Comprehensive sentencing guidelines systems must include all offences. How violent crimes are handled will necessarily affect how other crimes are handled. If English policy-makers want to stabilize or reduce the prison population, they will have to reduce average sentences for violent crimes from current levels, or substantially reduce use of imprisonment for drug, property and other non-violent offences. *Justice for All* should have started the work of educating practitioners and the media about the need to reduce the severity of sentences for violent crimes. That will be a challenging political task, and it is not one to which a sentencing council composed mostly of judges will be well suited.

The fourth section discusses the issues that the various reports ducked about special sentencing provisions for dangerous offenders. Unless policy-makers want to authorize judges to be capricious in their decisions to deprive 'dangerous' offenders of their liberty, some hard decisions requiring intellectual honesty will have to be made. Policy-makers will have to specify a narrow set of crimes that are serious enough to trigger eligibility for dangerous-offender sentencing, the kinds of predicted harms that are serious enough to warrant taking preventive action, and the level of predictive accuracy in relation to sufficiently serious harms that will suffice to permit the state to deprive people of liberty.

Two chastening empirical findings are germane. First, serious violence is, thankfully, rare. It is a low-base-rate phenomenon, which makes it difficult to predict. Second, predictions of dangerousness are notoriously inaccurate. When prediction of serious violence is required, false positive predictions (mistaken predictions that people will commit violent acts who in fact will not) outnumber accurate predictions by at least two to one, but usually by five or six to one. Accurate predictions are easy if any crime counts. A person with seven or eight convictions of any crime has an 85–90 per cent likelihood of a future conviction for some crime. That's because drug offenders and nuisance property offenders commit crimes at extraordinarily high rates. Violence is different. It would be hard in principle to justify taking an offender's liberty, over and above what a current crime justifies, in order to prevent future violence, on the basis of prediction of commission of any but very serious violent crimes.

Violent crime in England and Wales

Victimization data show that violence in England and Wales declined during the 1990s. Police data on recorded crimes are not inconsistent with this, though they need some explanation before this becomes clear. It is thus understandable why Halliday and the White Paper gave relatively little attention to violence *per se*, but not why they gave so much attention to 'dangerous' offenders or why judges increased severity of sentences for violent crimes so markedly.

Demonstration of the decline in violence should start with victimization data. Table 6.2 shows British Crime Survey (BCS) estimates of violent crime incidents for selected years in the 1990s and up to 2001/02 for the three offences counted – common assault, wounding and robbery – and broken down into a typology based on victims' relationships with their attackers (domestic, acquaintance, stranger, muggings). The numbers fluctuate a good deal, because violence is a rare event and the BCS sample sizes typically have been too small to capture very many violent events. Annual samples started around 10,000 in 1981, rose to 19,400 in 1998, and were projected to reach 40,000 by 2001. Nonetheless, as Table 6.2 shows, estimated numbers of violent offences are down nearly across the board. The final columns show percentage changes from 1997 and 1999. Nearly all are negative numbers.

Recorded crime data show a less clear pattern but are consistent with the victimization data. Table 6.3 shows official data on recorded crimes for selected violent offences for selected years in the 1990s and through 2001–02. The numbers of completed and attempted murders fluctuated within a narrow band from 1995 through 2000/01, rising significantly only in 2001/02. Robberies also fluctuated within a narrow band, from 1995 through 1998–99, rising thereafter in large part because of increases in street robberies, especially of mobile phones (Simmons *et al.* 2002: 54).

Table 6.2 Violence victimization rates, 1991–2001/02[1]

Rates per 10,000 adults	1991	1995	1997	1999	2000	2001/02	% change 1997 to 2001/02	% change 1999 to 2001/02
Violence								
Common assault	432	718	599	563	487	421	*–30%***	*–25%***
Wounding	154	255	196	157	99	155	*–21%*	*–2%*
Robbery	45	83	82	98	73	85	*4%*	*–13%*
All BCS violence	651	1,046	897	832	669	679	*–24%***	*–18%***
Domestic violence	–	243	199	187	122	149	*–25%**	*–29%*
Acquaintance	–	446	401	297	207	210	*–48%***	*–29%***
Stranger	–	247	191	231	257	216	*13%*	*–6%*
Mugging (robbery and snatch theft)	64	103	102	112	83	104	*2%*	*–8%*

[1]Statistical significances of changes are indicated by a single asterisk for significance at the 10% level and double asterisk at the 5% level (two tailed tests).

Source: Simmons *et al*. 2002: table 3.02

Table 6.3 Recorded violent crimes, 1991, 1995 to 2001/02

Numbers

Offence	1991	1995	1996	1997	1997/ 98	1998/ 99	1998/ 99*	1999/ 00*	2000/ 01*	2001/ 02*
Homicide	725	745	679	739	748	750	750	766	850	886
Attempted murder	555	634	674	652	661	676	676	750	708	858
Threat or conspiracy to murder	4,712	7,044	8,533	9,340	9,661	11,112	11,212	13,434	14,064	13,648
Wounding or other act endangering life	9,408	10,445	12,169	12,531	12,833	13,960	14,006	15,135	15,662	16,537
Rape of a female	4,045	4,986	5,759	6,281	6,523	7,139	7,132	7,809	7,929	9,008
Rape of a male	–	150	231	347	375	502	504	600	664	735
Robbery	45,323	68,074	74,035	63,072	62,652	66,172	66,835	84,277	95,154	121,375

*per revised classification scheme
Source: Simmons *et al*. 2002: table 3.04

For a variety of less serious violent crimes, Table 6.3 shows large increases in crimes recorded by the police. Most of this however, is the product of changes in reporting by citizens and recording by police. Both reporting and recording of sexual crimes have increased in most Western countries since the mid-1970s as a consequence of deliberate efforts to have them prosecuted more vigorously and to increase awareness of and official actions against spousal, acquaintance and date rape. These efforts have also increased reporting and recording of assaults as reporting of domestic violence incidents has increased. In the United States, much of the run-up in recorded rates of aggravated assault is attributed to substantial increases in reporting and recording of domestic assaults (Blumstein and Beck 1999). Besides this, Western countries have been characterized by declining tolerance of violence, which has increased reporting and recording of assaults that in earlier times would not have been considered worth bothering with.

Most specialists in criminal statistics agree that heightened concern about crimes against women and reduced tolerance for violence have increased rates of sexual and violent crime as shown in police statistics, but no one knows exactly how much. There are, however, two good ways to demonstrate that changes in reporting and recording practices create misleading impressions that violent crime rates are increasing.

Table 6.4 shows BCS data on citizens' reporting of violent victimizations to the police from 1981 to 2000. Numbers fluctuate significantly, because of the relatively small numbers of violent incidents reported. Nonetheless, the figures on percentages of victimizations reported to the police show a clear and steady increase. This can be seen especially clearly by comparing the first (1981), fourth (1991), and final (2000) columns of the table. Reporting rates were higher for every offence in 1991 than in 1981 and higher again in 2000 than in 1991. For every offence shown, rates in the final column are much higher than in the first. Victims are reporting substantially higher percentages of their victimizations to the police than in earlier times.

Table 6.5 makes the same point, in a more complex way but to my mind more compellingly in relation to recording practice. Part A shows numbers of recorded murders (think of them as successful attempts; row 1), attempted murders (row 2), conspiracies/threats to commit murder (row 3), and woundings/endangerings (row 4). For simplicity I sometimes refer to the last two categories as 'very serious assaults'. From 1991 to 1999, the numbers of successful and attempted murders fluctuated within fairly narrow bands (the same pattern also characterized robbery during the same years), but the numbers of threats/conspiracies and of wounding/endangerings more than doubled.

Table 6.4 Percentage BCS incidents reported to the police. British Crime Survey, selected years, 1981–2000

	A. Basic definitions								
	1981	1983	1987	1991	1993	1995	1997	1999	2000
Common assault	25.1	30.5	32.5	25.5	23.2	34.4	31.2	29.0	39.2
Wounding	40.2	59.6	43.3	47.7	53.2	39.2	45.1	58.2	68.2
Robbery	46.5	39	43.9	47.2	48.3	55.9	55.9	30.8	54.1
	B. Salient characteristics								
Domestic	19.6	13.3	46.3	23.4	21.6	30	26.3	31.3	43.4
Acquaintance	25.2	35.3	34	29.1	32	36.7	34.5	36.8	37.5
Stranger	35.2	46.8	30.3	37.5	39.1	38.5	44.8	38.3	47.8
Mugging	37.8	41.6	44.9	47.2	45.7	59.5	54.7	32.7	52.8

Source: Kershaw *et al.* 2001: table A2.4

Part B of Table 6.5, shows that there was steady bracket creep in relation to police-recorded violence throughout the period it covers. While it is possible that some of the increased levels of very serious assaults result from increased levels of reporting by victims, most violent acts as serious as these likely would have been reported at any time. The police, however, appear to have been relabelling assaults upwards in severity.

Part B shows the changing percentages of homicides among broader categories of violent crime. When the ratios of deaths (row 1, part A) to successful and unsuccessful attempts (rows 1 and 2) are calculated, they remain similar for all years shown. Of all events that might be thought of as attempted murder, over the entire period 53.3 per cent resulted in death. The death rate ranges from 50 to 58 per cent and shows no trend, merely fluctuating around the mean.

When a similar calculation is made of deaths (row 1) as an outcome of successful and unsuccessful attempted homicides and threats/conspiracies combined (rows 1–3), the pattern is very different. The death probability slowly but steadily declines throughout the decade and is less than half as high in 2000/01 as it was in 1990. A similar pattern holds for deaths (row 1) calculated as an outcome of successful and attempted homicides, threats/conspiracies and woundings/endangerings combined (rows 1–4).

There is no plausible explanation other than labelling bracket creep

Table 6.5 Murder ratios to violent offences, 1990–2000/01

	A. Recorded violent crimes												
	1990	1991	1992	1993	1994	1995	1996	1997	97/ 98	98/ 99	98/ 99*	99/ 00*	00/ 01*
1. Murder	669	725	687	670	726	745	679	739	748	750	750	766	850
2. Attempted murder	476	555	568	661	651	634	674	652	661	676	676	750	708
3. Threat/conspiracy to murder	4,162	4,712	5,487	5,638	6,844	7,044	8,533	9,340	9,661	11,112	11,212	13,434	14,064
4. Wounding/endangering life	8,920	9,408	10,741	10,701	11.033	10,445	12,169	12,531	12,833	13,960	14,006	15,135	15,662
	B. Ratios of murders to other violent crimes												
Total 1+2	1,145	1,280	1,255	1,331	1,377	1,379	1,353	1,391	1,409	1,426	1,426	1,516	1,558
1÷(1+2)	**.584**	.566	.547	.503	.527	**.540**	.502	.531	.531	.526	.526	.505	**.546**
Total 1+2+3	5,307	5,992	6,742	6,969	8,221	8,423	9,886	10,731	11,070	12,538	12,638	14,950	15,622
1÷(1+2+3)	**.126**	.121	.102	.096	.088	**.088**	.069	.069	.068	.060	.059	.081	**.054**
Total 1+2+3+4	14,227	15,400	17,483	17,670	19,254	18,868	22,055	23,262	23,903	26,498	26,644	30,085	31,284
1÷(1+2+3+4)	**.047**	.047	.039	.038	.038	**.039**	.031	.032	.031	.028	.028	.025	**.027**

*per revised classification scheme
Source: Home Office 2001c: table 2.15

for the declining death ratios. The quality of emergency medical care cannot have changed very much over a decade and, if it had, it would have reduced all the ratios including that of deaths to successful and unsuccessful attempted homicides. If that ratio did not change, none of the others should have. Death is a probabilistic outcome of violent crimes just as car accidents and deaths are probabilistic outcomes of miles driven. Unless the circumstances of potentially lethal incidents change markedly, death ratios should not change.

Think about instruments of death as an example. All else equal, an attack with fists is less likely to be life-imperilling than an attack with a knife, which is in turn less likely to be life-imperilling than an attack with a 22-calibre revolver, which in successive turns is less likely to be life-threatening than attacks with 45-calibre revolvers, semi-automatic weapons and hand grenades. If there were some reason to suppose that life-threatening incidents were becoming less dangerous, for example, changing firearms' availability or lethality, that might explain declining death ratios. It wouldn't, however, explain why the most basic ratio held steady and the others declined. Concerning firearms, the trend is in the other direction with firearms use in crime increasing (Simmons *et al.* 2002: fig. 3.2). If more assault situations involve guns, the death ratio should be increasing, not decreasing.

So the best explanation for why death ratios are declining is that police are relabelling formerly less seriously regarded crimes as very serious assaults. This isn't surprising. A rising sea lifts all boats. If English society generally is becoming less tolerant of violence (and more likely to report it to the police), it would be surprising if police officers weren't also becoming less tolerant of violence and therefore inclined to take some alleged crimes more seriously than in earlier times.

The key conclusion of this section is that violent crime is not rising and hasn't been for a long time (except for anomalies like mobile-phone robberies, and they will decline as technological fixes take hold). There is no reason to doubt this conclusion. Nearly all Western countries likewise experienced stable and declining crime rates in the 1990s (van Kesteren *et al.* 2000; Farrington *et al.* 2004). There is nothing in English crime trends to suggest why violence generally or 'dangerous offenders' should be regarded as worsening problems.

Sentencing violent offenders in England and Wales

English sentencing for violent crimes became much harsher during the

1990s, just as did sentencing in the United States. An already-classic article on the US experience by Blumstein and Beck (1999) showed that during the 1980s the major drivers of increasing prison populations were vast increases in prison sentences for drug offenders and across-the-board increases in percentages of offenders receiving custody. The numbers of cases being processed grew and the percentages of those receiving prison sentences grew, for a compounding effect. In the 1990s, drug offenders remained an important factor, but the major drivers were substantial increases in the lengths of prison sentences; admissions to prison declined. In brief, the cause in the 1980s was increases in prison admissions and in the 1990s it was increases in sentence lengths.

I'm not aware of comparable analyses in England. Readily available data on English sentencing, however, suggest that both factors – increased probabilities of prison sentences and longer sentences – are contributing to rising prison populations. Table 6.6 shows data on sentences imposed on adults in English courts for indictable violent, sexual and robbery offences in 1989 and 1999. Consistent with declining crime rates, the raw numbers of people sentenced for violent and sexual offences each fell by more than 40 per cent. The number of sentences for indictable robbery increased by about 15 per cent.

From those data one might expect that the numbers of people sentenced to prison for violent and sexual crimes would have fallen substantially by 1999, and the number sentenced for robbery would have increased slightly, assuming business as usual. What happened instead is that the percentage of violent offenders receiving custody grew from 18 to 34 per cent, and the absolute number of violent offenders sent to prison increased, rising from 8,485 to 10,085. For sexual offenders likewise. The percentage receiving prison sentences increased from 35 to 66 per cent and the absolute number increased from 2,330 to 2,509.

From these data one might expect that average sentence lengths would have fallen because of what is known as the 'marginal offender effect'. From a fixed pool of, say, 5,000 offenders, it is reasonable to assume that judges would send to prison those who had committed the most serious offences or had the most extensive criminal records or who for some other reason appeared to be dangerous. If the size of the pool did not change but the number sentenced to prison grew from 1,000 to 2,000, the incremental 1,000 would on average have committed less serious offences, had less extensive records, or appeared less dangerous. For these reasons, the second thousand imprisoned offenders should on average receive shorter sentences than the first

Table 6.6 Defendants aged 18 and over sentenced to imprisonment, indictable offences, 1989 and 1999

	Violence			
	Total sentenced	Total custody	% custody	Average sentence (in months)
1999	29,978	10,085	34%	16.2
1989	48,195	8,485	18%	15.5
Difference	–18,217	+1,600	+16%	+0.7 mo
	Sexual			
	Total sentenced	Total custody	% custody	Average sentence (in months)
1999	3,822	2,509	66%	37.8
1989	6,704	2,330	35%	35.4
Difference	–2,882	+179	+33%	+2.4 mo
	Robbery			
	Total sentenced	Total custody	% custody	Average sentence (in months)
1999	3,613	3,180	88%	40.5
1989	3,166	2,690	85%	41.2
Difference	+477	+490	+3%	–0.7 mo

Source: Home Office 2001b: app. 2, tables 2, 4

thousand. The marginal offender is the next one to be sent to prison and in 1999 can be expected to be less culpable or dangerous than the average of those who preceded him.

Thus when the number of sentenced sex offenders fell from 6,704 to 3,822, if there were no change in sentencing severity and 35 per cent received prison sentences, as in 1989, 1,338 should have been sent to prison. Instead, 66 per cent (2509) of that smaller number of offenders received prison sentences. On marginal-offender reasoning, the average sex offender sent to prison in 1999 was a considerably less culpable or dangerous person than was the average imprisoned sex offender in 1989. A similar analysis applies to violent offenders, whose probability of receiving a prison sentence nearly doubled from 18 to 34 per cent.

The marginal-offender analysis suggests that average lengths of prison sentences should have fallen significantly for both violent and sex offenders (but not for robbery, for which the imprisonment rate grew only a little from 85 to 88 per cent). After all, the average offender should be a less culpable or scary person than in earlier times.

Instead, sentencing severity increased. As noted in the introduction to this chapter, the average sentence for violent offenders increased a little, from 15.5 to 16.2 months, and the average sentence for sex offenders increased by a slightly larger amount, from 35.4 to 37.8 months. These may seem like small absolute increases, but if the average sentenced case was much less serious in 1999 than in 1989, these may be very large increases for more serious crimes.

There are other indications of increased severity. Table 6.7 shows data on long sentences (three years or more) for 1989 and 1999. The marginal-offender hypothesis supports a prediction that the percentages of violent and sexual (but not robbery) defendants receiving long sentences should have fallen greatly by 1999. Instead, the percentages receiving long sentences increased for all three offences. So did the number of life sentences.

There are limitations in the analyses in this section,[1] but they do demonstrate that sentencing severity for violent (including sexual) crimes grew substantially in England in the 1990s, and was a major contributor to the record increase in prison population.

Sentencing and corrections policies for violent offences

The Halliday report and the White Paper made significant mistakes when they neglected to emphasize declining violence rates and to discuss trends in criminal violence and violence prevention generally. Instead, both devoted their primary attention to exceptional high-media-coverage cases and special policies for dangerous offenders. By definition these are highly unusual cases that provoke strong emotions and punitive reactions. That can be regretted in its own right but also, and more, because it creates stereotypes of violence based on horrifying cases. To many people, no punishment is too severe for a horrifying case and cost considerations are irrelevant. Most credible research on

Table 6.7 Sentence lengths, violence, sexual, robbery, 1989 and 1999

	Violence			
	No. custody	No. 3 yrs +	% 3 yrs+	No. life
1999	10,085	1,752	17.4%	328
1989	8,485	1,201	14.2%	188
Difference	+1,600	+551	+3.2%	+140
	Sexual			
	No. custody	No. 3 yrs +	% 3 yrs+	No. life
1999	2,509	1,115	44.4%	71
1989	2,330	1,005	43.1%	19
Difference	+179	+110	+1.3%	+52
	Robbery			
	No. custody	No. 3 yrs +	% 3 yrs+	No. life
1999	3,180	1,797	56.5%	36
1989	2,690	1,392	51.7%	1
Difference	+490	+405	+4.8%	+35

Source: Home Office 2001b: app. 2, tables 4 and 5

public opinion and attitudes about crime shows that the public is badly misinformed and that opinions are often based on stereotypes created by sensational cases featured in the news and entertainment media (Roberts *et al.* 2003).

Severity of sentencing for violent crimes has increased substantially since 1989, and, as US experience shows, there is no natural stopping point. If today's norms are always the starting point for proposals for increased severity, the English prison population will continue growing indefinitely. If policy-makers, citizens and the media think of horrific crimes when they hear the word 'violence', policy will continue to be emotion – rather than knowledge – driven.

The reality is that violence is exceedingly common and mundane, and is mostly not very serious. The British Crime Survey estimated that there were 2,891,000 violent incidents experienced by adults in 2001/02 (Simmons *et al.* 2002: 47), and very few of these were the kinds of horrifying crimes that attract media attention. Of those not reported to the police, 91 per cent were not reported because the incident was 'trivial' or because victims would rather deal with it themselves (Simmons *et al.* 2002: table 3.06).

So what should Halliday and the White Paper have proposed and discussed?

- They should have devoted considerable time to the good news that violence is down.
- They should have documented the substantial increases in sentences for violent crimes and the roles those increases have played in prison population increases.
- They should have closely examined sentencing patterns for violent crimes to document what kinds of crimes receive what kinds of sentences, and to establish for which kinds of crimes sentences have increased and by what amounts.
- They should have identified particularly pressing violence problems that need new or radical solutions, and explained why.
- They should have examined existing laws to determine which if any should be retained.
- They should have examined the literature on violence prevention (e.g., anger management, alcohol's role in violence, etc.) and proposed ways that judges could build preventive measures into sentences and that probation and prison officials could incorporate preventive measures into their programming.

Closer, more sustained and less stereotyped attention to violence was needed for four reasons. First, insofar as treatment programmes can reduce the incidence of violence, government should invest in programming and related evaluations and technical assistance, and encourage judges and corrections officials to use prevention programmes in all appropriate cases.

Second, arguments needed to be made that explained why some violence problems needed new solutions and others did not. The principal recommendations of both Halliday and *Justice for All* and the major violence-related provisions in the Criminal Justice Bill and Act involve special measures for dangerous offenders, but there is no discussion of why they are needed. Are there more such offenders than before? Are existing laws and practices, if sensibly and efficiently applied, inadequate, and in what respects? There is no evidence to support any such claims.

Third, existing laws should have been examined to determine whether they were achieving their goals. Halliday, for example, reported that many whom he interviewed expressed continuing opposition to mandatory life sentences, and suggested that successful implementation of his proposals might provide occasion to consider their repeal. He took no view in the matter but implied his sympathy with the critics. Neither this nor retention of discretionary life sentences was discussed on the merits in either Halliday or the White Paper. They should have been. The evidence is overwhelming that mandatory penalties seldom achieve their putative deterrent goals. The evidence is equally overwhelming that both mandatory penalties and discretionary life sentences often cause injustice in individual cases (Tonry 1996: chap. 4).

Fourth, the keystone proposals for creation of a sentencing guidelines council and promulgation of comprehensive sentencing guidelines are predicated (though the reports fail to discuss this) on sensible handling of violent crimes. Most sentencing councils to date have recognized that sentencing guidelines drafting is a zero-sum game. The prison pie is a finite resource and a larger slice for one crime, for example, white-collar crime, implies a smaller slice for another. Similarly, if increasing amounts of prison space are to be used for offenders who breach conditions of community penalties, other uses must be reduced. Every responsible sentencing council has had to make such trade-offs.

Given the sizeable recent increases in violent offenders' odds of going to prison and in the lengths of sentences they receive, reduction in severity of sentences for violent offenders will be an important option for the Sentencing Council. Halliday hinted at this in one proposal: 'The proposed new sentencing guidelines should not assume that existing norms for sentence length would be equally punitive in the new framework or that the existing custody rate would be equally appropriate' (Home Office 2001b: 64). The White Paper and the Criminal Justice Bill and Act accepted Halliday's sentencing council proposal but the odds that it will be acted on in relation to violent crimes would be better if the White Paper had expressly discussed the subject and endorsed the proposal in relation to violence.

Sentencing policy for 'dangerous' violent offenders

The only significant proposals in the White Paper concerning violence are sketchy and appear almost to be an afterthought to proposals concerning sex offences and offenders (Matravers and Hughes 2003). The principal proposal is that, in addition to existing laws permitting discretionary life sentences for some violent and sex offences, and mandating life sentences for persons receiving a second conviction for designated violent offences, a new law is required that creates indeterminate sentences for some violent offenders and allows for extended – possibly life-time – supervision after release from prison.

Halliday's proposal, which the White Paper said it accepted, is more fully elaborated. He proposed a 'special' sentence for offenders presenting high risks of re-offending and serious harm, and who have been convicted of one from a list of designated offences. Qualifying offenders sentenced to prison terms above a threshold (Halliday proposed four years) would serve at minimum half of the term, like all other long-sentence prisoners. Unlike other offenders who must then be released, however, affected prisoners would be held at the pleasure of the Parole Board and would be released before expiration of their term only when the Parole Board decided. Affected offenders could also be subjected to up to ten years community supervision following release.

The White Paper proposal is much vaguer than Halliday's. It has three interrelated main features, all offered in hopelessly vague terms. First, it will apply, variously, to 'dangerous', 'dangerous and sexual', 'violent and sexual', and 'dangerous, sexual, and violent' offenders. Lawyers' definitional issues abound. Do 'dangerous' and 'violent' mean the same thing in classifying offenders? Or is 'dangerous offenders' the operative category in which violent and sexual offenders are sub-categories. More importantly, will qualifying violent (or dangerous) offenders be defined in relation to the crimes of which they were convicted, or will 'dangerous' be a clinical assessment? If the latter, on what basis will the assessment be made?

'Violent offence' in section 31(1) of the Criminal Justice Act 1991 (now part of the PCCS Act 2000) was defined as 'an offence which leads, or is intended or likely to lead, to a person's death or to physical injury to a person [and includes arson]'. This is a hopelessly broad definition that could encompass all crimes resulting in death or physical injury whether intended or even foreseeable or not. Unless judges are to be given almost unlimited discretionary powers, the term 'dangerous violent offender' needs to be defined narrowly and by statute.

Second, the White Paper contemplated dangerousness assessments by someone ('offenders ... who are nevertheless assessed as dangerous') but it doesn't say by whom or according to what criteria. Halliday helpfully pointed out that dangerousness should entail high risks of both 're-offending' and of 'serious harm', and referred to existing statutes that provided at least for-instance formulations. Risk-prediction technology for minor offences is powerful. It's easy to predict accurately that an active nuisance offender will re-offend. Risk prediction for serious violence, including serious sexual violence, is not powerful and is plagued by high false-positive rates (Monahan 2004). The White Paper discussed none of this.

Third, the White Paper provided that affected offenders be held during the second, indeterminate part of their sentences until the 'Parole Board was completely satisfied that the risk had sufficiently diminished'. 'Completely satisfied' is a nonsensical standard that could never be met.

Fourth, the White Paper and the ensuing Bill both delegated predictive decisions about dangerousness to trial judges to make seat-of-the-pants decisions. More politely phrased, the Bill contemplates 'clinical' predictions of dangerousness based on the judge's experience and his or her application of that experience to individual cases. Unfortunately, nearly 50 years of research have demonstrated that clinical predictions of dangerousness are less often accurate than are actuarial predictions based on quantitative analyses of the conduct of large numbers of people (Meehl 1954; Monahan 1981; Matravers and Hughes 2003; Monahan 2004).

Finally, neither the White Paper nor Halliday said anything about evidentiary standards, about rights of notice, confrontation, representation by counsel and fact-finding before a 'special' sentence could be imposed, or about the kinds of evidence that might be considered in deciding whether exceptionally high risks of re-offending and serious harm had been shown.

The Act backs off somewhat from the White Paper's rhetoric and contains provisions resembling Halliday's recommendations, though they are broader and more susceptible to the overuse and misuse Halliday feared.

The overbreadth takes three forms. First, the provisions are triggered by convictions of any of 65 specified violent offences and 88 specified sexual offences, only some of which could possibly count as acts typically committed by dangerous offenders.

Second, the Act creates a number of presumptions against liberty. Any adult offender who is charged with any of the 153 specified offences, and who was previously convicted of any of them, is assumed to present a serious risk to the public of serious harm (section 229). Once imprisoned under the dangerous-offender provisions, an offender is not, like other prisoners entitled to automatic release on licence on serving half the sentence, but may be held until it expires unless the Parole Board 'is satisfied that it is no longer necessary for the protection of the public that the prisoner should be confined' (section 247).

Third, the basic finding of dangerousness is to be made by a judge, according to vague criteria: 'whether there is a significant risk to members of the public of serious harm' (section 229). Everything we know about predictions of dangerousness instructs that judges tend to overpredict and that judges' individualized clinical predictions are less accurate than are statistical predictions.

* * * *

The White Paper's and the Bill's proposals concerning violent offenders were underdeveloped and under-explained. Halliday concluded his discussion of special sentences for dangerous offenders by pointing out that 'More thought needs to be given to the options than has been possible in this review.' The drafters of the White Paper and the Criminal Justice Act, however, appear to have given the subject considerably less thought than Halliday did.

The White Paper, for example, never explained why new legislation was needed atop the discretionary and mandatory life sentences that are already available for sentencing people convicted of violent crimes. Nor does it explain why those laws remain necessary. There is no discussion of newly discovered violence problems that warrant heroic solutions, nor of a crisis of serious violence.

Footnote

1 Most importantly is the possibility of a 'selection bias', which simply means that the criteria for selection of cases that are processed as indictable offences may have changed in a systematic way. For example, less serious cases may have been screened out, with the result that by 1999 only much more serious cases than the 1989 average were being handled as indictable offences. Overaggregation is another problem. The sentencing data are broken into much too broad and amorphous categories. Policy- making would be considerably better informed if an analysis like that in Blumstein and Beck (1999) were to be carried out in order to establish the factors that have most contributed to prison population increase.

Chapter 7

What's next

Four times before I've written books comparable to this one, examining major crime control and sentencing policy issues. All dealt with the United States. Each concluded with a chapter that proposed ways out of problems that the book discussed. That's a reasonable thing to do in a country containing nearly 60 different criminal law jurisdictions and in which the national government handles only a tiny fraction of criminal cases and 6 per cent of prisoners. A government in one of those jurisdictions, or governments in several, may pay attention and something might happen as a result. In England and Wales, there is only one criminal law jurisdiction and the government in power has just enacted a package of 'reform' proposals that were several years in the making.

The time hardly seems right to propose new initiatives, especially ones that would require repeal of legislation just passed. Chapters 4 and 5 of this book offer concrete proposals for reducing racial disparities in the English criminal justice system and developing a meaningful, comprehensive set of sentencing guidelines. Chapters 1 and 6 canvass a wide range of over-broad, anti-civil-liberties provisions of the Criminal Justice Act 2003, concerning 'dangerous' offenders and procedures aimed at minimizing wrongful convictions, for which the only appropriate action in a liberal society is repeal and reconsideration.

None of those proposals is likely to be adopted or to be taken seriously, but there is irony in this. The proposals are mostly modest and evidence-based. Many experienced Home Office civil servants, and many experienced criminal justice practitioners, would favour many of them. The most senior ministers, however, do not, but for reasons not of policy but of politics.

I've personal experience of this dissonance between the views of civil servants and officials and their political masters. Not long ago, I gave a presentation to a committee composed of heads of criminal justice agencies, ministers and senior civil servants. Answering a question concerning community penalties and prison populations, I explained how other jurisdictions had successfully dealt with a particular problem. Nodding heads showed that many in the room thought what I said made sense. I then said that England could do something similar if only there were the political will. Rolling eyes suggested there is not.

The scene I described is a remarkable one because it reveals an extraordinary gap between the most senior Labour ministers and the officials who run major agencies. For whatever reasons, the current government has opted for what Sir Anthony Bottoms called 'populist punitiveness' as its criminal justice policy platform, even though most experienced practitioners believe many current policies are unsound. There is, for example, nearly unanimous agreement among judges, probation officers, prison officials, criminal lawyers and researchers that mandatory minimum sentences are a bad idea. The government doesn't care that opposition to mandatory penalties is 'widely supported by informed opinion in the country at large'.

The words in inverted commas were uttered, ruefully, by Peter Hain, the leader of the Commons, in response to criticism of recent Labour proposals to abolish the post of Lord Chancellor and create a supreme court: 'Every time a Labour government proposes a sensible constitutional reform, widely supported by informed opinion in the country at large, the Tories oppose it' (Watt and White 2003: 2).

One can understand Peter Hain's frustration, but wonder why 'informed opinion in the country at large' concerning the criminal justice system is so completely and cavalierly disregarded by the Labour government. On the small issues, evidence sometimes counts. On the big ones, emulation of American crime-control policies and politics is the order of the day.

References

Andenaes, J. (1974) *Punishment and Deterrence*. Ann Arbor: University of Michigan Press.

Anderson, D.C. (1995) *Crime and the Politics of Hysteria: How the Willie Horton Case Changed American Justice*. New York: Cowan.

Ashworth, A. (2000) *Sentencing and Criminal Justice*, 3rd edn. London: Butterworths.

Ashworth, A. (2001) 'The Decline of English Sentencing and Other Stories', in M. Tonry and R.S. Frase (eds), *Sentencing and Sanctions in Western Countries*. New York: Oxford University Press.

Auld, Lord Justice (2001) *Report of the Review of the Criminal Courts of England and Wales*. London: HMSO.

Benn, H. (2003) *Stakeholder Consultation: Summary of Responses to Hilary Benn's Letter of 6 September*. London: Home Office, Strategy and Finance Unit.

Bennett, T., Holloway, K. and Williams, T. (2001) *Drug Use and Offending: Summary Results From the First Year of the NEW-ADAM Research Programme*. Home Office Research Findings 148. London: Home Office.

Bingham, Sir T. (1996) 'The Courts and the Constitution', *Kings College Law Journal*, 7, 12–26.

Blumstein, A. and Beck, A. (1999) 'Population Growth in U.S. Prisons, 1980–1996', in M. Tonry and J. Petersilia (eds), *Prisons*. Chicago: University of Chicago Press.

Blumstein, A., Cohen, J. and Nagin, D. (eds) (1978) *Deterrence and Incapacitation: Estimating the Effects of Criminal Sanctions on Crime Rates*. Washington DC: National Academy Press.

Blumstein, A., Cohen, J., Martin, S. and Tonry, M. (1983) *Research on Sentencing: The Search for Reform*, 2 vols. Report of the National Academy of Sciences

Panel of Sentence Research. Washington DC: National Academic Press.
Blunkett, D. (2004) *Reducing Crime-Changing Lives. The Government's Plans for transforming the management of offenders.* London: Home Office.
Boerner, D. and Lieb, R. (2001) 'Sentencing Reform in the Other Washington', in M. Tonry (ed.), *Crime and Justice – A Review of Research*, vol. 28. Chicago: University of Chicago Press.
Bottoms, A.E. (1995) 'The Philosophy and Politics of Punishment and Sentencing', in C.M.V. Clarkson and R. Morgan (eds), *The Politics of Sentencing Reform.* Oxford: Clarendon Press.
Bowling, B. and Phillips, C. (2001) 'Prosecution and Sentencing', in *Racism, Crime and Justice.* Longman Criminology Series. Harlow: Longman.

Carrow, D. (1984) 'Judicial Sentencing Guidelines: Hazards of the Middle Ground', *Judicature*, 68, 161–71.
Carter, P. (2003) *Managing Offenders, Reducing Crime – A new approach.* London: Home Office, Strategy Unit.
Clifford, G. (1996) 'Norway: A resolutely welfare-oriented approach', in P. Cavadino (ed.), *Children Who Kill: An examination of the treatment of juveniles who kill in different European countries.* Winchester: Waterside Press.
Cook, P. (1980) 'Research in Criminal Deterrence: Laying the Groundwork for the Second Decade', in M. Tonry and N. Morris (eds), *Crime and Justice: An Annual Review of Research*, vol. 2. Chicago: University of Chicago Press.
Cook, P. and Ludwig, J. (2000) *Gun Violence: The Real Costs.* New York: Oxford University Press.

Denman, S. (2001) *Race discrimination in the Crown Prosecution Service.* London: HMSO.
Dodd, V. (2000) 'Top Judge Attacks Prison "Cancer"', The *Guardian*, 28 December 2000.
Doob, A. (1995) 'The United States Sentencing Commission: If you don't know where you are going, you might not get there', in C. Clarkson and R. Morgan (eds), *The Politics of Sentencing Reform.* Oxford: Clarendon Press.
Doob, A. and Webster, C. (2003) 'Sentencing Severity and Crime: Accepting the Null Hypothesis', in M. Tonry (ed.), *Crime and Justice: A Review of Research*, vol. 30. Chicago: University of Chicago Press
Downes, D. and Morgan, R. (2002) 'The Skeletons in the Cupboard: the Politics of Law and Order at the Turn of the Millennium', in M. Maguire, R. Morgan and R. Reiner (eds), *The Oxford Handbook of Criminology*, 3rd edn. Oxford: Oxford University Press.
Dunbar, I. and Langdon, A. (1998) *Tough Justice – Sentencing and Penal Policies in the 1990s.* London: Blackstone.
Dworkin, R. (1988) *Law's Empire.* Cambridge, MA: Harvard University Press.

Edsall, T. and Edsall, M. (1991) *Chain Reaction: The Impact of Race, Rights, and Taxes on American Politics*. New York: Norton.

Farrington, D.P. (2002) 'Key Results from the First 40 Years of the Cambridge Study in Delinquent Development', in T.P. Thornberry and M. Krohn (eds), *Taking Stock of Delinquency*. New York: Kluwer/Plenum.

Farrington, D.P., Langan, P. and Tonry, M. (eds) (2004) *Cross-national Studies in Crime and Justice*. Washington DC: Bureau of Justice Statistics, US Department of Justice.

Faulkner, D. (2001) *Crime, State and Citizen: A Field Full of Folk*. Winchester: Waterside Press.

Flood-Page, C., Campbell, S., Harrington, V. and Miller, J. (2000) *Youth Crime: Findings from the 1998/99 Youth Lifestyles Survey*. Home Office Research Study 209. London: Home Office.

Frankel, M. (1973) *Criminal Sentences: Law without Order*. New York: Hill & Wang.

Frase, R. (2004) 'Sentencing Policy in Minnesota', in M. Tonry (ed.), *Crime and Justice: A Review of Research*, vol. 32. Chicago: University of Chicago Press.

Gaes, G., Flanagan, T., Motiuk, L. and Stewart, L. (1999) 'Adult Correctional Treatment', in M. Tonry and J. Petersilia (eds), *Prisons*. Chicago: University of Chicago Press.

Garland, D. (2001) *The Culture of Control*. Oxford: Oxford University Press.

Griset, P. (1991) *Determinate Sentencing: The Promise and the Reality of Retributive Sentencing*. Albany NY: SUNY Press.

Harrington, V. and Mayhew, P. (2001) *Mobile Phone Theft*. Home Office Research Study 235. London: Home Office.

Home Office (1990) *Crime, Justice, and Protecting the Public*. Cm. 965. London: HMSO.

Home Office (2000) *Criminal Statistics on Race and the Criminal Justice System*. London: Home Office, Research, Development and Statistics Directorate.

Home Office (2001a) *Criminal Justice: The Way Ahead*. Cm. 5074. London: Home Office.

Home Office (2001b) *Making Punishments Work*. Report of a Review of the Sentencing Framework for England and Wales (July 2001) (The Halliday report.). London: Home Office Communication Directorate.

Home Office (2001c) *Criminal Statistics, England and Wales, 2000*. London: Home Office.

Home Office (2002a) *Justice for All*. Cm. 5563. London: Home Office.

Home Office (2002b) *Justice for All: Responses to the Auld and Halliday Reports*. London: Home Office.

Home Office (2003) *Prison Statistics, England and Wales, 2001*. Cm. 5743. London: Stationery Office.

Hood, R. (1992) *Race and Sentencing*. Oxford: Oxford University Press.

Hough, M., Jacobson, J. and Millie, A. (2003) *The Decision to Imprison: Sentencing and the Prison Population*. London: Prison Reform Trust.

Hough, M. and Roberts, J.V. (1998) *Attitudes to punishment: findings from the British Crime Survey*. Home Office Research Study No. 179. London: Home Office.

Hough, M. and Mitchell, D. (2003) 'Drug Dependent Offenders and "Justice for All"', in M. Tonry (ed.), *Confronting Crime: Crime Control under New Labour*. Cullompton: Willan Publishing.

Jareborg, N. (1995) 'The Swedish Sentencing Reform', in C. Clarkson and R. Morgan (eds), *The Politics of Sentencing Reform*. Oxford: Clarendon Press.

Jareborg, N. (1998) 'Why Bulk Discounts in Multiple Offence Sentencing?', in A. Ashworth and M. Wasik (eds), *Fundamentals of Sentencing Theory: Essays in Honour of Andrew von Hirsch*. Oxford: Oxford University Press.

Jones, P. (2002) 'The Halliday Report and Persistent Offenders', in S. Rex and M. Tonry (eds), *Reform and Punishment: The Future of Sentencing*. Cullompton: Willan Publishing.

Kershaw, C. and colleagues (2001) *The 2001 British Crime Survey: First Results. England and Wales*. London: Home Office.

Kommer, M. (1994) 'Punitiveness in Europe: A Comparison', *European Journal on Criminal Policy and Research*, 2, 29–43.

LaFranière, P. (1992) 'Governor's Camp Feels His Record on Crime Can Stand the Heat', *Washington Post*, 5 October, p. A6.

Lappi-Seppälä, T. (2001) 'Sentencing and Punishment in Finland: The Decline of the Repressive Ideal', in M. Tonry and R.S. Frase (eds), *Sentencing and Sanctions in Western Countries*. New York: Oxford University Press.

Lovegrove, A. (1989) *Judicial Decision-making, Sentencing Policy, and Numerical Guidelines*. New York: Springer-Verlag.

Macpherson, Lord (1999) *The Stephen Lawrence Inquiry*. Cm. 4262.I. London: HMSO.

Martin, S. (1984) 'Interests and Politics in Sentencing Reform: The Development of Sentencing Guidelines in Pennsylvania and Minnesota', *Villanova Law Review*, 29, 21–113.

Matravers, A. (ed.) (2003) *Sex Offenders in the Community*. Cullompton: Willan Publishing.

Matravers, A. and Hughes, G. (2003) 'Unprincipled Sentencing? The Policy Approach to Dangerous Sex Offenders', in M. Tonry (ed.), *Confronting Crime: Crime Control under New Labour*. Cullompton: Willan Publishing.

Mayhew, P. and van Dijk, J. (1997) *Criminal Victimisation in Eleven Industrialized Countries: Key Findings from the 1996 International Crime Victims Survey*. The Hague: Dutch Ministry of Justice.

McClintock, F.H. and Avison, N.H. (1968) *Crime in England and Wales*. London: Heinemann.

McDonald, D. and Carlson, K. (1993) *Sentencing in the Federal Courts: Does Race Matter?* Washington DC: U.S. Department of Justice, Bureau of Justice Statistics.

Meehl, P.E. (1954) *Clinical Versus Statistical Prediction: A Theoretical Analysis and a Review of the Evidence*. Minneapolis MI: University of Minnesota Press.

Monahan, J. (1981) *The Clinical Prediction of Violent Behavior*. Washington DC: U.S. Government Printing Office.

Monahan, J. (2004) 'The Future of Violence Risk Management', in M. Tonry (ed.), *The Future of Imprisonment*. New York: Oxford University Press.

Morris, N. and Tonry, M. (1990) *Between Prison and Probation*. New York: Oxford University Press.

Muncie, J. (2002) 'Policy Transfers and What Works: Some reflections on comparative youth justice', *Youth Justice*, 1(3): 27–35.

Nagin, D. (1998) 'Criminal Deterrence Research at the Outset of the Twenty-first Century', in M. Tonry (ed.), *Crime and Justice: A Review of Research*, volume 23. Chicago: University of Chicago Press.

Padfield, N. and Crowley, R. (2003) 'Procedural and Evidential Protections in the English Courts', in M. Tonry (ed.), *Confronting Crime: Crime Control under New Labour*. Cullompton: Willan Publishing.

Paveley, R. (2002) 'Child muggers behind rise in crime to be locked up', *Daily Mail*, 26 February.

Petersilia, J. and Turner, S. (1993) 'Intensive Probation and Parole', in M. Tonry (ed.), *Crime and Justice: A Review of Research*, vol. 17. Chicago: University of Chicago Press.

Phillips, K.P. (1970) *The Emerging Republican Majority*. Garden City NY: Anchor Books.

Prime, J., White, S., Liviano, S. and Patel, K. (2001) *Criminal Careers of those Born Between 1953 and 1968*. Home Office Statistical Bulletin 4/01. London: Home Office.

Radzinowicz, L. (1999) *Adventures in Criminology*. London: Routledge.

Reiner, R. (1992) 'Race, Crime and Justice: Models of Interpretation', in L. Gelsthorpe (ed.), *Minority Ethnic Groups in the Criminal Justice System*. Cambridge: Institute of Criminology.

Reiss, A.J., Jr., and Roth, J. (eds) (1993) *Understanding and Controlling Violence*. Washington DC: National Academy Press.

Reitz, K. (2001a) 'The Status of Sentencing Guidelines Reforms in the United States', in Tonry, M. (ed.), *Penal Reform in Overcrowded Times*. New York: Oxford University Press.

Reitz, K. (2001b) 'The Disassembly and Reassembly of U.S. Sentencing Practices', in M. Tonry and R.S. Frase (eds), *Sentencing and Sanctions in Western Countries*. New York: Oxford University Press.

Roberts, J. and Smith, M.E. (2003) 'Custody Plus, Custody Minus', in M. Tonry (ed.), *Confronting Crime: Crime Control under New Labour*. Cullompton: Willan Publishing.

Roberts, J., Hough, M., Stalans, L. and Indermahr, D. (2003) *Penal Populism and Public Opinion: Lessons from Five Countries*. New York: Oxford University Press.

Rutherford, A. (1996) *Transforming Criminal Policy: spheres of influence in the United States, the Netherlands and England and Wales during the 1980s*. Winchester: Waterside Press.

Ryan, M. (2003) *Penal Policy and Political Culture in England and Wales*. Winchester: Waterside Press.

Savelsberg, J. (1994) 'Knowledge, Domination, and Punishment', *American Journal of Sociology*, 99, 911–43.

Simmons, J. and Dodd, T. (2003) *Crime in England and Wales 2002/2003*. London: Home Office Communication Development Unit.

Simmons, J. and colleagues (2002) *Crime in England and Wales 2001/2002*. London: Home Office.

Slevin, P. (2000) 'The Forgotten Issues; Democrats Neutralize GOPs Edge on Crime', *Washington Post*, 27 August 2000, p. A1.

Smith, D.J. (1994) *The Sleep of Reason: The James Bulger case*. London: Century.

Smith, D. (1997) 'Ethnic Origins, Crime, and Criminal Justice in England and Wales', in M. Tonry (ed.), *Ethnicity, Crime and Immigration*. Chicago: University of Chicago Press.

Smith, D. (2003) *The Nature of Personal Robbery*. Home Office Research Study No 254. London: Home Office.

Social Exclusion Unit (2002) *Reducing Re-offending by Ex-prisoners*. London: Deputy Prime-Minister's Office.

Stith, K. and Cabranes, J. (1998) *Fear of Judging: Sentencing Guidelines in the Federal Courts*. Chicago: University of Chicago Press.

Stratford, N. and Roth, W. (1999) *The 1998 Youth Lifestyle Survey*. London: Home Office.

Tak, P. (2001) 'Sentencing and Punishment in the Netherlands', in M. Tonry and R.S. Frase (eds), *Sentencing and Sanctions in Western Countries*. New York: Oxford University Press.

Tonry, M. (1991) 'The Politics and Processes of Sentencing Commissions', *Crime & Delinquency*, 37, 307–29.

Tonry, M. (1995) *Malign Neglect: Race, Crime, and Punishment in America*. New York: Oxford University Press.

Tonry, M. (1996) *Sentencing Matters*. New York: Oxford University Press.

Tonry, M. (ed.) (1997) *Ethnicity, Crime, and Immigration: Comparative and Cross-national Perspectives*. Chicago: University of Chicago Press.

Tonry, M. (1999) 'Why Are U.S. Incarceration Rates So High?', *Crime and Delinquency*, 45, 419–37

Tonry, M. (2002) 'Setting Sentencing Policy through Guidelines', in S. Rex and M. Tonry (eds), *Reform and Punishment: The Future of Sentencing*. Cullompton: Willan Publishing.

Tonry, M. (2004) *Thinking about Crime*. New York: Oxford University Press.

Tonry, M. and Farrington, D.P. (1995) 'Strategic Approaches to Crime Prevention', in M. Tonry and D.P. Farrington (eds), *Building a Safer Society*. Chicago: University of Chicago Press.

Travis, A. (2002) 'Prison Crisis: Overcrowding: Tough on Crime, Tougher on Jails', *The Guardian*, 13 July 2002, p. 4.

US Surgeon General (2001) *Youth Violence: A Report of the Surgeon General*. Washington DC: US Public Health Service.

van Dijk, J. and Mayhew. P. (1992) *Criminal Victimisation in the Industrialised World*. The Hague: Ministry of Justice, Directorate for Crime Prevention.

van Dijk, J., Killias, M. and Mayhew, P. (1990) *Experiences of Crime across the World: Key Findings from the 1989 International Crime Victim Survey*. Deventer: Kluwer.

van Kesteren, J., Mayhew, P. and Nieuwbeerta, P. (2000) *Criminal Victimisation in Seventeen Industrialised Countries*. The Hague: Ministry of Justice.

von Hirsch, A., Knapp, K.A. and Tonry, M. (1986) *Sentencing Commissions and their Guidelines*. Boston MA: Northeastern University Press.

Von Hirsch, A., Bottoms, A. Wikström, P-O and Burney, E. (1999) *Criminal Deterrence and Sentence Severity: An Analysis of Recent Research*. Oxford: Hart.

Wasik, M. (2001) 'How Should Guidelines be Produced? How should they be Monitored?' Paper prepared for QMW Public Policy Seminar on Policy and Practice for Sentencing, 23 October 2001.

Watt, N. and White, M. (2003) 'Blair Refuses', The *Guardian*, 18 June, p. 2, cols 3–4.

Weigend, T. (2001) 'Sentencing and Punishment in Germany', in M. Tonry and R.S. Frase (eds), *Sentencing and Sanctions in Western Countries*. New York: Oxford University Press.

Whitman, J.Q. (2003) *Harsh Justice: Criminal Punishment and the Widening Divide between America and Europe*. New York: Oxford University Press.

Windlesham, Lord D. (1996) *Responses to Crime, vol.3, Legislating with the tide*. Oxford: Clarendon Press.

Woolf, Lord (1999) Foreword to *Adventures in Criminology*, by Sir Leon Radzinowicz. London: Routledge.

Wright, R. (2002) 'Counting the Cost of Sentencing in North Carolina, 1980–2000', in M. Tonry (ed.), *Crime and Justice – A Review of Research*, vol. 29. Chicago: University of Chicago Press.

Young, A. (1996) *Imagining Crime: Textual outlaws and criminal conversations.* London: Sage Publications.

Zimring, F. and Hawkins, G. (1998) *Crime is Not the Problem: Lethal Violence in America.* New York: Oxford University Press.

Index